T0323885

ALAN BALL

CONVERSATIONS

TELEVISION CONVERSATIONS SERIES
DAVID LAVERY, GENERAL EDITOR

ALAN
BALL
CONVERSATIONS

Edited by Thomas Fahy

UNIVERSITY PRESS OF MISSISSIPPI / JACKSON

www.upress.state.ms.us

The University Press of Mississippi is a member of the Association of American University Presses.

First printing 2013

∞

Library of Congress Cataloging-in-Publication Data

Alan Ball : conversations / edited by Thomas Fahy.
    pages cm — (Television conversations series)
  Includes index.
  ISBN 978-1-61703-877-8 (cloth : alk. paper) — ISBN 978-1-61703-878-5 (ebook)
  ISBN 978-1-4968-5798-9 (paperback)
  1. Ball, Alan, 1957——Interviews. 2. Television writers—United States—Interviews.
3. Screenwriters—United States—Interviews. 4. Dramatists, American—20th cen-
tury—Interviews. I. Fahy, Thomas Richard editor of compilation.
  PS3552.A4543Z46 2013
  812'.54—dc23
  [B]   2013014726

British Library Cataloging-in-Publication Data available

CONTENTS

INTRODUCTION

Alan Ball never intended to write for television. He majored in theater at Florida State University and in the early 1980s moved to New York to become an actor and playwright. While living in a Brooklyn brownstone with three other guys and a dog named Mom, he soon discovered that waiting around for auditions wouldn't pay the rent (Brough). He started looking for a job and eventually landed a position as an art director for a trade publication. The nine-to-five routine of corporate America, however, felt stifling for Ball. He longed to be part of an artistic community in the city. So with the help of several friends from college, he started a theater company—Alarm Dog Repertory. This small group would produce several of Ball's early plays, including *Power Lunch* (1989), *Your Mother's Butt* (1990), and *Bachelor Holiday* (1991), which later became the inspiration for his short-lived sitcom *Oh, Grow Up* (1999). At the same time, some of his other plays were starting to reach a wider audience, including *The M Word*, which premiered at the Lucille Ball Festival of New Comedy in 1991, and *Made for a Woman* (1993). But it was the Manhattan Class Company's successful production of *Five Women Wearing the Same Dress* (1993) that caught the attention of Hollywood.[1] A television talent scout saw the play, and soon Marcy Carsey and Tom Werner hired Ball as a script editor and staff writer for *Grace Under Fire*. Ball recalls that at the time he had never seen a television spec script and "didn't even watch TV" (Royal). But in 1994 he decided to give television writing a chance.

Alan Ball has repeatedly—and colorfully—described his experiences with *Grace Under Fire* (1994–1995) and *Cybill* (1995–1998): "It was really frustrating. It was infuriating. [. . .] It was like being a member of the court of some mad monarch who was completely insane and power hungry and crazy and doing completely destructive things to the country, but nobody could say anything" (Champagne). In large part, Ball's resentment came from the fact that so much of the final product was shaped by personal politics and commercial demands: "You just really couldn't be too invested in it because everything got changed daily based on the whims of certain people. If you were invested in it, it was just too painful" (Chumo). So Ball spent these years doing formulaic writing, or "factory work" as he has called it, and feeling disconnected from his art.

After three seasons on *Cybill*, Ball began to pursue a career in feature films. He didn't want to be pigeonholed as a comedy television writer, and he desired to write something that he could feel passionate about, something meaningful. With the support of his new agent, Ball returned to a project that he had started as a play in the early 1990s—a project inspired in part by the media frenzy surrounding Joey Buttafuoco's trial. It wasn't until the summer of 1997, after years of disillusioning work for television, that Ball was ready to tell the story of Lester Burnham's midlife crisis as a film. In his original conception, Lester—a character inspired by Buttafuoco—"was a man who was shut down. Who had given up. Who [didn't] really have any passion for his own life. [. . .] That [was] something that [had] been happening to me, both artistically and in life in general."[2] This was the genesis of *American Beauty*. The film received five Academy Awards in 1999, including Best Picture, Best Original Screenplay (Alan Ball), Best Actor (Kevin Spacey), and Best Director (Sam Mendes). Ball has joked that winning this award changed his status in Hollywood: "People all of a sudden felt like I knew what I was talking about" (Brough). Winning this award also changed the television industry's attitude about what Ball was capable of as a writer.

Soon after the success of *American Beauty*, Carolyn Strauss (former senior vice-president for original programming and current president of Home Box Office Entertainment) proposed an idea for a television show about a family-run funeral home and America's relationship with death. Ball hesitated at first, but after his sitcom *Oh, Grow Up* was cancelled, he wrote the pilot episode of *Six Feet Under* (2001–2005). For Ball, *Six Feet Under* was a cathartic experience: "I've been able to work out a lot of my own fears about death and the finality of death [. . .]. And working on the show has allowed me [. . .] to open myself up to living more fully, surprisingly enough. And I do think that is the purpose of grief. When you've lost someone close to you, you lose a part of yourself, and you have to grieve for that and you have to let go of it" (Carugati). Much of the anguish that Ball worked through in the series *Six Feet Under* stemmed from the traumatic loss of his sister when he was thirteen. On her twenty-second birthday, Mary Ann Ball was driving Alan to his piano lesson. She pulled out into a blind intersection and hit an oncoming car. The accident broke her neck, killing her instantly. As Ball recounts in the book *Six Feet Under: Better Living Through Death*, her death "[sliced] my life in two: everything before the accident, and everything after."[3]

Ball wasn't able to write about this loss until *Six Feet Under*. In the opening moments of the pilot episode, a man named Nathaniel Fisher dies suddenly in a car accident, and his death divides the show in half—everything before the accident, and everything after. Mr. Fisher's presence throughout the series (along with the other "clients" of the funeral home who appear to the family) also serves as a reminder that the dead are still with us. This show gave Ball the opportunity to transform his own experiences with grief into art and to confront the culture of avoidance surrounding death in America. "I actually spent many years holding the grief back. [. . .] But . . . we live in a culture that goes out of its way to deny mortality" (Chumo). Ball further explains in the DVD commentary about the pilot, "One of the reasons I wanted to set the show in LA is because LA is the world capital of the denial of death." Perhaps young Nate Fisher best summarizes Ball's point at his father's funeral: "No! I refuse to sanitize this anymore . . . [Death] is a goddamn part of life, and you can't really accept it without getting your hands dirty." Week after week, the series got our hands dirty. It depicted the sudden, ugly, heartbreaking, and painful reality of death. It delved into the psychological and emotional hardship of loss. And it did so through characters that struggled, suffered, failed, and tried again in their quest for healing.

Ball didn't have any directing experience before *Six Feet Under*, but he had learned a great deal from Sam Mendes while working on *American Beauty*: "I spent a lot of time watching the way Sam and Connie [Conrad Hall] were setting up the shots and watching the way Sam worked with the actors because that's why I wanted to be on the set, I [had] aspirations to direct myself [. . .]. So I wanted to kind of soak up the experience as much as I could" (Royal). Ball brought this experience, as well as his rich visual sense as a writer, to *Six Feet Under*, and in 2002 he earned an Emmy for directing the pilot episode.

At the end of *Six Feet Under*, Ball shifted his attention back to live theater and feature films. He drafted *All That I Will Ever Be*—a play that was produced by the New York Theatre Workshop in 2007—and he found the experience quite liberating: "To have a character start talking and talk for a really long time because what they're trying to express is complicated and they have all kinds of different feelings about it. So I really enjoyed that" (Fahy). *All That I Will Ever Be* tells the story of Omar, a man who works both as an electronics salesman and a gay hustler in Los Angeles. Omar copes with his fear of intimacy through lying and constructing various "exotic" identities as a prostitute. These identities, such as Farouk, the Arabian Stallion, also enable him to satirize American bigotry toward the Middle East.

The play's depiction of racism shares similarities with Alicia Erian's novel *Towelhead*, which Ball adapted for the screen and directed in 2007. The film tells the coming-of-age story of Jasira, a thirteen-year-old Lebanese-American girl who lives in a Houston suburb and experiences statutory rape, physical abuse, misogyny, and racism fueled by the first Gulf War (August 1990–February 1991). Given the subject matter of *Towelhead*, it is not surprising that every major Hollywood studio passed on the film. Ball struggled to get financing for the project, and the film (once released[4]) caused controversy. Like *American Beauty*'s portrait of sexuality, violence, and the artificiality of suburbia, *Towelhead* communicates equally uncomfortable truths about American culture.

Even Jasira's use of a tampon outraged some critics, which Ball finds amusing: "We are a patriarchal culture, and female sexuality is pretty terrifying. The fact that I go to screenings of this movie with smart, urban, educated people, and they still gasp at the site of a tampon, is hilarious to me" (Doughton).

While working on *All That I Will Ever Be* and *Towelhead*, Ball was talking with HBO about a new television series based on the vampire novels of Charlaine Harris. Ball viewed *True Blood* as very different from his previous work: "When I pitched it to HBO for the first time I said, 'This is popcorn television'" (Gross 2008). After focusing on characters struggling with self-denial and repression in *Six Feet Under*, Ball turned to a world of excess in *True Blood*. He explains in the DVD commentary for the pilot episode (which he wrote and directed in 2008) that "the show is not about the control of emotions that might feel dangerous. If anything the show is about total lack of control all of the time." *True Blood*—like Harris's novels—is set in a world where vampires have come out of the coffin, so to speak, to live openly among humans and to lobby for equal rights. The series' exploration of the human fascination with and repulsion for vampires (particularly in regard to sexuality) centers on the romantic relationship between Sookie Stackhouse, a quirky Southern girl with telepathy, and a world-weary vampire named Bill Compton. Part of Sookie's attraction is visceral, and part of it stems from the fact that—because he is dead—she cannot hear his thoughts. The show also raises provocative questions about prejudice, linking America's history of intolerance for interracial marriage and homosexuality with the bigotry experienced by vampires.

Ball ultimately views the show as being "about the terrors of intimacy, about breaking that wall that keeps you separate and safe from a sometimes savage and dangerous world; and letting another person in, ultimately, is a terrifying act" (Gross 2008). He articulates this theme explicitly through Sookie's grandmother, Adele Stackhouse, in the episode "Mine": "Well, it is scary—opening your heart up to somebody." In this sense *True Blood* shares much in common with Ball's other works in that individual repression and inauthenticity often come from a fear of intimacy. Even the excesses of Lester Burnam's regression into adolescence in *American Beauty* and of David Fisher's reckless behavior while coming out as homosexual in the first season of *Six Feet Under* parallel the risks that many characters in *True Blood* take in their desire for intimacy. And it almost goes without saying that *Six Feet Under*'s preoccupation with the fear of mortality is central to *True Blood* as well.

In 2012, Ball announced that he would step down as executive producer of *True Blood*, in part, to pursue two projects: a new television series and a film. The first season of *Banshee*, which aired on Cinemax in early 2013, follows the adventures of an ex-convict who has assumed the identity of a sheriff in Banshee, Pennsylvania. This disguise facilitates his ongoing criminal activities and helps him hide from his dangerous past. Ball is the showrunner and one of the executive producers for the show, which was created by novelists Jonathan Tropper and David Schickler. Ball has also completed writing his next feature-length film, *What's the Matter with Margie?* The film is scheduled for release in 2014 and will star Elizabeth Banks as Margie.

The interviews reprinted in *Alan Ball: Conversations* span a twelve year period from *American Beauty* to the present. Because Ball continues to write for theater, film, and television, I have selected several interviews that include his thoughts on all three genres. Ball views each one in very different terms: "Well, theater is more language-oriented—you can luxuriate in words, in rhythm, in the music and poetry of language. Film is like a dream—you can tell a story visually, with really beautiful images and symbols and subconscious currents and mythic moments. TV for me is like a novel because you can continue to develop a story over hours and hours and hours. You can really get to know the characters and be with them and grow with them" (Lucia). For fans of Alan Ball's television writing, his role on the upcoming series *Banshee* means that we will have several new chapters in the "novel" of Alan Ball to look forward to.

I want to thank all of the interviewers, publications, and organizations for granting permission to reprint these interviews. I am especially grateful to James McLeod for sharing his recording of the Wheeler Centre interview with me and to the Wheeler Center and the Archives for American Television for their generosity. I am also grateful for the support of Long Island University and the University Press of Mississippi.

This volume would not have been possible without the tireless efforts of my research assistant, Laura Angyal. Her professionalism and hard work are evident on every page. I also wish to thank Tatyana Tsinberg who patiently endures the traumas of every book project and always manages to help me cross the finish line.

Finally, many thanks to Alan Ball for years of inspiring theater, television, and film and for his support of this book.

TF

NOTES

1. For more on Ball's early career in the theater, see Thomas Fahy's "Introduction" in *Considering Alan Ball: Essays on Death, Sexuality, and the American Dream* (Jefferson, NC: McFarland Press, 2006), 1–16.

2. Sharon Waxman, "Alan Ball's Life After Death," *Washington Post*, May 26, 2002.

3. Alan Ball, *Six Feet Under: Better Living Through Death* (New York: Pocket, 2003), 79.

4. *Towelhead* premiered at the Toronto Film Festival on September 8, 2007. It was released in the United States one year later (September 26, 2008).

CHRONOLOGY

1957—Alan Ball born on May 13 in a suburb outside of Atlanta, Georgia.

1970—Gets in a car accident with his sister, Mary Ann, on her twenty-second birthday. She was driving Alan to a piano lesson when she crashed into an oncoming car. She died instantly.

Early 1980s—Attends the theater program at Florida State University.

1986—He leaves college without graduating and moves to New York City to be a playwright. He starts Alarm Dog Repertory Theater Company with several friends from college.

1989—*Power Lunch* is produced by Alarm Dog Repertory.

1990—*Your Mother's Butt* is produced by Alarm Dog Repertory.

1991—*Bachelor Holiday* is produced by Alarm Dog Repertory. This play would become the inspiration for his later sitcom *Oh, Grow Up*.

1991—*The M Word* premieres at the Lucille Ball Festival of New Comedy.

1993—*Five Women Wearing the Same Dress* produced by the Manhattan Class Company and catches the attention of a Hollywood talent scout.

1994—Offered a position on the writing staff of the sitcom *Grace Under Fire* (ABC, 1994–1995) and moves to Los Angeles.

1995—Joins the writing staff of the sitcom *Cybill* (CBS, 1995–1998).

1999—Writes and co-produces *American Beauty*, which earns over $350 million worldwide.

1999—Creates and produces sitcom *Oh, Grow Up* (ABC, September–December), based on his experiences as a gay man living with heterosexual roommates in New York. The network aired seven of the thirteen episodes before cancelling the show.

2000—Receives Academy Award in Best Original Screenplay category for *American Beauty*. The film earned four additional Academy Awards: Best Picture, Best Director (Sam Mendes), Best Actor (Kevin Spacey), and Best Cinematography.

2001—Creates television drama *Six Feet Under* (HBO, 2001–2005) about the Fisher family and their funeral home business in Los Angeles.

2002—Receives Emmy for Outstanding Directing for a Drama Series for the pilot episode of *Six Feet Under*.

2007—Returns to the theater with the premiere of his play *All That I Will Ever Be* with the New York Theatre Workshop.

2007—Directs and writes the screen adaptation of Alicia Erian's novel *Towelhead*.

2008—Creates television show *True Blood* (2008–2012) based on *The Southern Vampire Mystery* series by Charlaine Harris.

2012—Leaves *True Blood* and becomes executive producer and showrunner for *Banshee*, an HBO/Cinemax production.

2014—Tentative release date for Ball's new feature-length film, *What's the Matter with Margie?*

WORKS FOR THEATER, FILM, AND TELEVISION

PLAYS

The following plays were written and performed in the early 1980s for the General Nonsense Theater Company in Florida.

Cherokee County
Frostproof

The following plays were written and performed for Alarm Dog Repertory in New York (1986–1994).

The Two Mrs. Trumps (1986/1987)
Power Lunch (1989)
Your Mother's Butt (1990)
Bachelor Holiday (1991)
The M Word (1991)
Made for a Woman (1993)
Five Women Wearing the Same Dress (1993)
The Amazing Adventures of Tense Guy (1994)

The following play was first produced by the New York Theatre Workshop.

All That I Will Ever Be (2007)

FILMS

***American Beauty* (1999)**
Writer: Alan Ball
Director: Sam Mendes
Cast:
Kevin Spacey—Lester Burnham

Annette Bening—Carolyn Burnham
Thora Birch—Jane Burnham
Wes Bentley—Ricky Fitts
Mena Suvari—Angela Hayes
Chris Cooper—Colonel Frank Fitts, USMC
Peter Gallagher—Buddy Kane
Allison Janney—Barbara Fitts
Scott Bakula—Jim Olmeyer
Sam Robards—Jim Berkley

Towelhead (2008)
Writer: Alan Ball (adaptation based on the novel by Alicia Erian)
Director: Alan Ball
Cast:
Summer Bishil—Jasira Maroun
Chris Messina—Barry
Maria Bello—Gail Monahan
Peter Macdissi—Rifat Maroun
Gemmenne de la Peña—Denise
Robert Baker—Mr. Joffrey
Aaron Eckhart—Travis Vuoso
Carrie Preston—Evelyn Vuoso
Chase Ellison—Zack Vuoso

What's the Matter with Margie? (2014)
Writer: Alan Ball
Director: Daniel Minahan

TELEVISION

Grace Under Fire (**ABC, 1993–1998**)
Created by Chuck Lorre
Series Writer: Alan Ball, 1994–1995
Cast:
Brett Butler—Grace Kelly
Casey Sander—Wade Swoboda
Kaitlin Cullum—Libby Kelly
Dylan Sprouse—Patrick Kelly
Cole Sprouse—Patrick Kelly
Dave Thomas—Russell Norton
Julie White—Nadine Swoboda

Cybill (CBS, 1995–1998)
Created by Chuck Lorre
Series Writer: Alan Ball, 1995–1998
Cast:
Cybill Shepherd—Cybill Sheridan
Christine Baranski—Maryann Thorpe
Alicia Witt—Zoey Woodbine
Alan Rosenberg—Ira Woodbine
Tim Maculan—Waiter
Dedee Pfeiffer—Rachel Blanders
Peter Krause—Kevin Blanders

Oh, Grow Up (ABC, 1999)
Created by Alan Ball
Cast:
Stephen Dunham—Hunter Franklin
David Alan Basche—Norris Michelsky
John Ducey—Ford Lowell
Rena Sofer—Suzanne Vandermeer
Neisha Trout—Chloe Sheffield
Freddy Rodriguez—Deke

Six Feet Under (HBO, 2001–2005)
Created by Alan Ball
Cast:
Peter Krause—Nate Fisher
Michael C. Hall—David Fisher
Frances Conroy—Ruth Fisher
Lauren Ambrose—Claire Fisher
Freddy Rodriguez—Federico "Rico" Diaz
Mathew St. Patrick—Keith Charles
Rachel Griffiths—Brenda Chenowith
Jeremy Sisto—Billy Chenowith
Lili Taylor—Lisa Kimmel Fisher
Richard Jenkins—Nathaniel Fisher

True Blood (HBO, 2008–present)
Created by Alan Ball (based on the novels of Charlaine Harris)
Cast:
Anna Paquin—Sookie Stackhouse
Stephen Moyer—Bill Compton
Sam Trammell—Sam Merlotte

Ryan Kwanten—Jason Stackhouse
Rutina Wesley—Tara Thornton
Chris Bauer—Andy Bellefleur
Nelsan Ellis—Lafayette Reynolds
Carrie Preston—Arlene Fowler
Jim Parrack—Hoyte Fortenberry
Alexander Skarsgård—Eric Northman
Kristin Bauer van Straten—Pam De Beaufort
William Sanderson—Sheriff Bud Dearborne

Banshee **(HBO/Cinemax, 2013)**
Created by Jonathan Tropper and David Schickler
Executive Producers: Alan Ball, Greg Yaitanes, Peter Macdissi, Jonathan Tropper and David Schickler
Cast:
Antony Starr—Sheriff Lucas Hood
Ulrich Thomsen—Kai Proctor
Ivana Milicevic—Anastasia
Frankie Faison—Sugar Bates
Hoon Lee—Job
Rus Blackwell—Gordon Hopewell

ALAN BALL
CONVERSATIONS

American Beauty: An Interview with Alan Ball

PETER N. CHUMO II / 2000

From *Creative Screenwriting*, January–February 2000. Reprinted by permission of Peter N. Chumo II.

Alan Ball was born and raised around Atlanta, Georgia. He majored in theater with an emphasis in acting and playwriting at Florida State University and then moved to New York, where he worked as an art director for *Adweek* and *Inside PR* magazines. While he did some acting and directing, he found his calling as a writer. His 1993 off-Broadway production, *Five Women Wearing the Same Dress*, attracted the attention of TV producers, who offered him a job in Los Angeles writing for the sitcom *Grace Under Fire*, which led to other work in television. He wrote *Cybill* for three seasons, and is the creator, head writer, and executive producer of the recent sitcom *Oh, Grow Up*.

American Beauty is Ball's first produced screenplay, but it was a long time in coming. He says that he "had been thinking about these characters and this particular story for years on and off." And had even tried writing it as a play. Finally, he wrote it as a screenplay and garnered the attention of Steven Spielberg, who loved it and bought the script for DreamWorks. The film, directed by Sam Mendes and starring Kevin Spacey and Annette Bening, has received some of the best reviews of 1999, many of which single out Ball's amazing writing.

Q: Can you tell me a little bit about yourself, especially as a writer?
A: I was a playwright living in New York, and I had been writing plays and directing and even doing a little acting here and there in theater companies that I had formed with other friends of mine from college in both Florida and New York. I wrote a play that was produced off-Broadway in 1993 called *Five Women Wearing the Same Dress*. And I got an offer to be a television writer based on that play, which was kind of surprising 'cause I had never even thought about that. I figured, "Sure, what the heck," and moved out to LA and spent a year on *Grace Under Fire*, which was in a lot of ways one of the most

educational experiences in my life. It was also pretty miserable. I went from there to spend three seasons on *Cybill*, writing screenplays on the side. I wrote an adaptation of my play, I did an assignment for Warner Brothers, and then I wrote *American Beauty* on spec.

Q: Did your theatrical or television backgrounds prepare you for *American Beauty*, or was that just a separate project?
A: They led to it in the sense that I became a better writer. I was in my third season on *Cybill*, and I just really felt like I was doing factory work. Not that I wasn't taking my work seriously, but I had no connection to it.

Q: Is that the nature of writing for TV?
A: No, because I'm writing for TV now, and I have a real deep connection to the stuff I'm writing. It was just the nature of what it took to survive on that show. You just really couldn't be too invested in it because everything got changed daily based on the whims of certain people. If you were invested in it, it was just too painful. You become a craftsman. And I really longed to be writing something that I could pour myself into and get kinda lost in and that I felt meant something, even just to me as the writer, because I had gotten used to that during my years as a playwright. I actually had just switched agents, and I went to UTA [United Talent Agency] because I said I don't want to be pigeonholed as a TV writer, I want to have a features career as well. So my new features agent said to me, "I need a spec. I need a new script 'cause these other scripts of yours have been floating around town and people know them, and I need something new that I can take out." And I said, "Okay, I'll write a spec." I pitched three ideas to him, two of which were fairly standard romantic comedies, and the third one was *American Beauty*, which was really kinda difficult to pitch because it's not a high-concept movie. And to my great surprise, he said, "Yeah. I think that's the one you should write." And I said, "Really? Why?" He said, "'Cause that's obviously the one you have the most passion about." And that was true. It was a story and characters that had been in my head for years. I had tried to write a play back in the early nineties about these characters, and it just didn't work. And I realized later it's because it was meant to be a movie. I think that's really the only way to tell that story.

Q: What was the initial inspiration for the screenplay?
A: Well, there were several inspirations for the screenplay. I was very fascinated by the Amy Fisher trial. I felt like there was a real story underneath the media hype that I'm sure was way more fascinating and way more tragic than any that we could see from just the media coverage. In the first draft of *American Beauty*, there's a big media trial in which Ricky and Jane are being tried for

Lester's murder because the videotape finds its way into the hands of the police. And then I had an encounter with a plastic bag one day in front of the World Trade Center. Also, I've had many jobs that I just detested, working for people that I had absolutely no respect for. A lot of Lester's story came from direct personal experience. I grew up in a household with a somewhat troubled father figure and a somewhat shut-down mother figure, so Ricky's household certainly resembles mine in ways. My father was never violent, but he was deeply conflicted in certain ways that are similar to the Colonel. So those are all the inspirations. There's no one specific thing.

Q: Can you tell me a little bit about the sale of the script? I've read that Spielberg fell in love with it and bought it for DreamWorks. Was there a bidding war before that?

A: There were other people interested. I can't remember exactly who they were, but they were smaller, independent-type producing entities. Personally, I never expected this script to sell. I thought people would think, "Oh, this is too fucked-up and weird," but I thought I would get some meetings out of it. I certainly never expected to sell it to DreamWorks, of all places, and I certainly never expected DreamWorks to make the movie in a way that I believe is exactly the way the movie should have been made. That's just narrow-mindedness on my part, but I sort of looked at DreamWorks and saw only big-budget, wide-appeal Hollywood stuff, and that's not what I felt the movie was. So I had met with about four or five different places, and then my agent called, and he said, "Steven Spielberg is reading the movie tonight." And I thought, "Well, that's funny." Then I found out the next day that he really liked it and that DreamWorks wanted to buy it. And I said, "That's really weird. I don't think DreamWorks is the right place to make this movie." And my agent said, "Well, go over there and meet with them." So I went over and met with Dan Jinks and Bruce Cohen, the producers who brought it into DreamWorks, and Glenn Williamson, whom I had known before, and Bob Cooper, who is no longer there. And I said, "You know my big fear is that you're gonna wanna iron the edge out of this script, to take out the darker stuff." And they said, "We won't. We promise we won't." And then on my way out to the car, Steven Spielberg was leaving his office, and Dan and Bruce called him over and introduced him to me. And I just kinda went, "Okay, just act really normal. You're about to meet Steven Spielberg. Just pretend this happens every day." I was so impressed with him. He's incredibly smart and very down-to-earth. He had some really wonderful things to say about the script. And I just instinctively went, "Well, this may be crazy, but I think this is the place to go." They also made me a co-producer on the movie and allowed me to have a really big part in the production of it, which is rare for writers, especially first-time writers.

Q: How did the project get set up from there? They got the director and then the actors followed? Were you involved in those decisions?

A: Yeah. Bruce and Dan promised me that they would keep me in the loop on everything, and they did. They were meeting directors all over town, and they would call me. I'm very opinionated. I would say, "Oh no no! I really don't like that idea!" Whether that had anything to do in their decisions I can't say, but they seemed to want my opinion about who was the right person. There were a couple of A-list directors interested for a while, even though I did not want this movie to be directed by a big A-list director because I knew the minute the budget started creeping upwards that then they'd really get nervous about content. Being a writer in movies is very different from being a writer in theater. If either one of them had chosen to do the movie, I probably would have been shown to the door. (laughs)

Film is definitely a director's medium. I think it's a writer's medium as well, but very rarely does a writer's work get translated to the screen as intact as mine did in this case, unless the writer is the director. In theater, you cannot make changes to the script without the writer's consent. The flip side, you know, is you can't make any money in the theater. (laughs)

Q: What kind of collaboration did you have with the director, Sam Mendes? I think it's especially interesting since both of you are first-time filmmakers and you both come from the theater.

A: It was great. When they mentioned Sam, I flew to New York to see *Cabaret*, and I was very impressed by it. Although it's very unlike *American Beauty* in a lot of ways, I could see that this was a man who had a keen visual sense. He had a real understanding of rhythm and pacing. He had a real understanding of lighting, of music, and using lighting and music to set moods, of really mining the material, not making the obvious choice as the way to approach material but looking for something a little deeper, a little more under the surface, which I thought was very appropriate to this particular script.

A lot of people's response to the script was "Oh, how could you ever like these people? They're so horrible." It's hard for me to understand that because I feel like when I wrote this movie, I loved these characters. They're not perfect, but, you know, who is? And none of them are malevolent. They're all doing what they're doing because they're lost and lonely and isolated, and it's heartbreaking. It's also, I think, kinda funny, in places. But ultimately it's quite sad, and Sam understood that. So I said, "I would love for this guy to direct the movie," but there was a long waiting period because a couple of the big names were still kind of interested, and they would have gone with them, I think, had they committed. But luckily both of those fell through, and they gave Sam the movie.

We worked together on the script a lot. We did a couple of passes on it before it went out to actors, then we did a couple of passes on it before we had our first table read. We had a two-week rehearsal period with the actors where we sat around a table and went through the script beat by beat and listened to their suggestions. There was some improvisation, some of which ended up in the shooting script, but not a lot. And all of this made the script stronger, more focused, and more cohesive.

Q: Did you do a lot of revising?
A: Yeah. I think by the time we finished shooting, there were ten different colors of pages in there, which I'm told is fairly standard, but there was no structural change. There was a decision after we shot the movie to excise the whole framing device at the trial. But it wasn't until we got it into the editing and looked at it that we all started to go, "This really doesn't seem necessary. This is too cynical." The movie is like its theme, it revealed itself to be something else than what we thought it was at first glance. To actually send those kids to jail and punish them for the murder, number one, was so heartbreaking after seeing what Wes [Bentley] and Thora [Birch] did in that story, and also it seemed unnecessarily cynical and really flew in the face of what's at the heart of the movie.

Q: In the first draft, when you're getting to the end and you have this great moment of transcendence with Lester's final speech, cutting to the trial seemed to get in the way of what the script was leading up to.
A: Yeah, it just wasn't necessary. I think when I wrote this, I was really angry, and so there was a lot of anger and cynicism that came out on the page. A lot of that stayed in, but ultimately I don't think the movie is about being angry or being cynical.

Q: I guess there's a remnant of that framing device in the pre-title scene where you see the videotape of the kids.
A: And it serves exactly the same purpose. You think, "Oh my God, these kids are gonna kill this guy," and gradually you realize that's not what happens.

Q: There are many impressive things about the script. One is the way you mix genres. It starts out as a family melodrama. It has elements of satire of American success and the American family. It moves effortlessly, it seems, from comedy to drama. It seems to end in tragedy and then really ends on a note of transcendence. How do you pull that off? Is that just something that happens unconsciously, or is that a real effort to get those things to blend without seeming jarring?

A: No, it wasn't a conscious effort. As a writer, I really like to straddle different tones because I just feel that's what life is like. I'm a person for whom humor is just such a major part of my outlook on the world that it's really hard for me to write something that doesn't have humor in it because I just get bored by it. I also think when you're able to really mix drama and comedy, it makes both of them stronger. If you've just come from a really funny scene and then something heartbreaking happens, it's got more impact and vice versa. If you're in the middle of some really disturbing scene and then someone says something really funny, you really want to laugh because of the tension. But it wasn't conscious. I didn't say, "I'm gonna mix a bunch of genres here," 'cause I don't think in terms of genres, I just think in terms of characters, and who are these people, what are their lives, and what's going on here?

Q: One theme in the screenplay is the conflict or tension between philosophies about looking at an image and going deeper. You have Buddy, the "Real Estate King," who talks about projecting an image of success. That's Carolyn's philosophy. And in opposition to that, you have Ricky, who looks behind things. He tries to go beyond appearances and even thinks he can see God by doing that. Was that an opposition you were setting up, or is that another one of those things that subconsciously just comes out in the writing?
A: I think it just came out subconsciously in the writing. I find the very image-conscious culture that we live in to be incredibly oppressive. I think I was writing about that, about how it's becoming harder to live an authentic life when we live in a world that seems to focus on appearance. It fascinates me, especially now in this media-driven age, that we're encouraged to purchase pre-packaged experience rather than have the experience ourselves. You know, you watch politicians debate, and, as if that wasn't phony enough, then there's a commentary afterwards where someone's going, "Well, I thought he looked really good. He handled himself. He seemed at ease." They don't even comment on what the person said. They're commenting on how he appeared as he said it. I just think that's totally whacked. And also living in a culture where every part of this country is becoming virtually indistinguishable from the other. You know, it's all Gap and Starbucks and Banana Republic, every corner of America is starting to look just like every other corner of America. For all of the differences between now and the fifties, in a lot of ways this is just as oppressively conformist a time. I think as human beings we have a spiritual need to live an authentic life, and that's becoming more and more difficult. You see so many people who strive to live the unauthentic life and then they get there and they wonder why they're not happy. We continue to have less and less community with each other; we continue to have more and more distances between ourselves and nature and the natural world. I guess I didn't really realize it when I sat down to write this, but these ideas are important to me.

Q: Lester seems to have the biggest character arc or transformation. What was the process in creating that character?

A: Well, I'm forty-two. I had my own little midlife crisis back when I was thirty-five because I'm such an overachiever. (laughs) But I think you do reach a point where you realize you have more of your life behind you than you do ahead of you. You start to reassess. All of a sudden things that seemed incredibly important at one point don't seem quite so important anymore. I think men especially yearn for the passion that they felt about life when they were younger. I do think you can maintain that passion throughout life, but when you basically work in a fluorescent-lit corporate environment in a cubicle for fourteen years, you're gonna have to put some of that passion on hold just to get through that. In a way, it was similar for me for what I had to do when I was working on those other sitcoms, where I just had to not care. Years of not caring is not good for the soul. I think there's a wake-up call in everybody's life, but it's an incredibly painful journey. Most world mythologies have some myth in which a hero goes into the underworld, and I think those myths are based on that psychological truth that people undergo this sort of transformation at some point in their lives. I feel like I'm equal parts Ricky and Lester. At least when I was writing it, I identified most strongly with those two characters. Everybody has a rebel inside them who wants to fight against the constraints of society. I think that's healthy, but I also think there are certainly instances where that becomes less than healthy, when you don't really know when to set limits. We are social beings, after all, and we do have to live in society and we can't just go through life satisfying every whim of our id. But what I like about Lester is he doesn't judge himself. A puritan would look at his visions of Angela and go, "Oh, that's disgusting, a middle-aged man lusting after a young girl like that." Without that judgment, I look at that and I go, "You know, here's a man who hasn't felt anything for years, and all of a sudden he's feeling something. That's not disgusting." His choice not to follow through with it redeems him, because she's not really the goal, she's the knock on the door. And I didn't even know that myself when I wrote the first draft of the script.

Q: Because in the first draft he does have sex with her.

A: Yeah, he does. And it's kind of like a completely horrible, disgusting thing. And I'm really glad that I realized the error of my ways. (laughs) Like I say, I was just so angry at the time I was writing the script. I was like, "Yeah! Do that!" But I very quickly realized that was not the way it should be.

Q: A lot of Lester's transformation seems to be about regressing to adolescence, but in a good sense. That is what empowers him. He becomes a frustrated schoolboy with Angela, he goes back to the music of his youth, he smokes pot, he gets the minimum-wage job at the burger place, and all that is sort of shocking and funny at the same time. But then when he gets to Angela at the end, when he gets what he thinks is the goal, he comes face-to-face with a real adolescent, with a real child.

A: And he's forced to become the father he can't be to his own daughter.

Q: Exactly. And that's what I thought was so beautiful about that, the way he cloaks her and he feeds her a sandwich. All that childhood regression was fun, but it leads him to being a father again.

A: Yes. And when he realizes that she is a child, he immediately, without a moment's hesitation, puts his own desires and needs aside and starts thinking about another person. That's like the tenet of so many spiritual disciplines, but we live in a culture where you're encouraged to be greedy and self-serving, and frankly we live in a culture that rewards that. Lester never could have gotten to that moment had he not gone on that weird, goofy journey.

Q: Another element in the first draft is revealing Colonel Fitts's homosexual experiences in the Marines and knowing that he is a repressed homosexual long before we find that out in the garage scene. Was the deletion there because you didn't want to reveal as much about that character so we could find out later?

A: Yeah. It just tipped too much. Also, no other character got a flashback, so structurally it was kind of odd.

Q: Yeah, it seemed like he was becoming the main character.

A: Right. It just wasn't right. I think I had to write that in my mind so I knew what happened to him. Because I believe that those two soldiers were in love and that he saw the person he loved die in front of his eyes, and I think he felt like he was being punished because being gay was a sin. A lot of times when you write, what comes out is what ends up being subtext, but you have to write it so that you know what it is. That was what happened in that particular case. The thing that people don't know is that he named Ricky after that boy.

Q: The power of denial seems to be a big theme in the film. Ricky has the line about his father when he tells Lester that his father actually thinks that he can buy all that video equipment with the catering jobs. He says, "Never underestimate the power of denial." And in retrospect that obviously applies to the Colonel's repressed homosexuality because it's that power of denial that's ultimately going to lead to Lester's demise. You have lines that fit the situation, but they foreshadow other things as well.

A: Right.

Q: Carolyn seems to be in denial about her relationship to her daughter. Angela has her own view of herself.

A: She is totally in denial. I think Carolyn and the Colonel are the two saddest characters. The Colonel has spent his entire life being unhappy because he bought into all the societal, fundamentalist crap and was unable to live a life as who he is. And Carolyn is totally missing the boat. One of the most haunting images to me is Lester's last vision of her and his remembrance of her on that amusement park ride when she used to be able to laugh like that. Everything is such effort. She just works so hard at everything, and she's so convinced that she's happy, but she's miserable. She's so miserable.

Q: One of the saddest moments starts out very funny. When they're on the sofa and Lester is trying to be romantic with her.
A: She can't go there.

Q: He's trying to reach out to her, and she just can't get beyond the material things.
A: There are a lot of people like that. I know a lot of people say she's a very cartoonish character, but I've certainly encountered people like that.

Q: The film is very beautiful visually, and I notice that the script itself is very visual. "Red" comes up a lot—the roses, the blood, of course, even the Burnhams' door is specified as red. Is red a symbol?
A: Red is a symbol of passion.

Q: It's Lester's passion that he's recovering?
A: For me. There's something dangerous about red. It's the color of blood. There's something violent about it. And there's also something incredibly beautiful about the color red. I can't say, "Yeah, the red door is a symbol of . . ." It's obviously a portal of some sort. I just knew when I was writing it and I was seeing this movie in my head, I just knew that that house had a red door, and I knew when Carolyn drives up in front of the house at the end that she sees the red door through the rain.

Q: Having a dead narrator and having him reveal at the beginning that he is going to die seems like a risky move. It's not something you had to do, but you chose to do, and I was wondering why? Some people might think you would lose your audience.
A: I think if you write from a point where you're thinking, "Am I going to lose the audience?" then you're not writing. That's marketing. I lost my sister. I was in a car accident when I was thirteen years old, and my sister died. My father died. I've lost a lot of friends to AIDS. I've had experiences with death, and I actually spent many years holding the grief back, and then I went through this sort of weird little nervous breakdown when I was living in New York right before I moved to LA—which was a horrible, horrible experience and also the

best thing that ever happened to me. There's a Buddhist notion about death: you can't really appreciate life until you fundamentally accept death and your own mortality. And I think that's very true. But I also think again we live in a culture that goes out of its way to deny mortality. The violence that we see in movies and everything doesn't have any consequences, it's sort of cartoonish. And we're so youth-obsessed, we so want to cover up and hide people who are aging, and it's very unhealthy. It's very unrealistic. Death is a fundamental truth of our existence. I feel like I'm a person who has accepted death because I've been forced to, and I fought that for many years, even after people I loved very much died. I certainly didn't set out to write a movie about how the acceptance of death is the only way you can really see life, but it is obviously something that was at the heart of this movie.

Q: The subject of death comes up again in the final draft with the funeral procession that Ricky and Jane see passing by. That scene doesn't appear in the first draft.
A: Yeah, that was actually a purely practical change. We were like two or three days behind on our schedule. The scene that that replaced was this big scene on a freeway.

Q: Yeah, a scene in Angela's car.
A: They said, "Can we do something cheaper that won't take as many days to shoot? And I just said, "Sure. Just as long as Ricky says the line, 'When you see something like that, it's like God looking right at you, and if you're real careful, you can look right back.' And Jane goes, 'What do you see?' and he says, 'Beauty.'" And they said, "Yeah, we can certainly do that." They wanted to cut that scene. They said it's not important. I said, "You're out of your fucking mind. It's one of the most important scenes in the movie!"

Q: That is one of the key lines.
A: Yeah. If any one line in this movie is the heart and soul of this movie, that is the line. So we figured out a way to do it that was much cheaper and only took a day to shoot. And I actually think it's better. There's a certain stillness in that scene. I love the way Sam shot it. There's a certain moment of breathing space 'cause that's that point in the movie where there's that one day where everyone's life just profoundly changes. I think that was a good call, but it was purely based on, "We don't want to spend this money. We can use three days to shoot a lot more other stuff than just this one scene."

Q: I think it's better for two reasons. One, the funeral procession prepares us for the ending, the ideas about death. And also I think it establishes an intimacy between Ricky and Jane. By taking Angela out of the scene, we can see

Ricky and Jane becoming closer so that, as they fall in love, it becomes more believable. We already know Angela's character.

A: Right. It's more of her being kind of snarky. (laughs) I think that was a really good choice.

Q: Any final thoughts about what you hope audiences will take away from the film?

A: I want audiences to take away from it what they take away from it. I know a lot of people really dislike the movie, and that's fine. I'm just glad it's not a movie that is just forgettable. You know, the minute you're out of the theater, it's like "Well, where do you want to go for drinks?" I just love that this is a movie that seems to make people think. Whether or not they like it is irrelevant. The most gratifying thing to me is that people do seem to have strong reactions to it.

American Beauty Screenwriter Alan Ball Conducts Case Study at the IFP/West Screenwriters Conference

SUSAN ROYAL / 2000

From InsideFilm.com, 2000. Reprinted by permission of Susan Royal.

IFP/West presented its annual screenwriting conference at the Writers Guild in Los Angeles on March 18–19. The keynote speaker, director David O. Russell (*Flirting With Disaster, Three Kings*), presented a preview of his hilarious "Indie Scale"—a numerical formula for evaluating the economic potential of an indie film—which he went on to deliver a week later to an appreciative audience of independent filmmakers at the IFP Independent Spirit Awards. Among the many panel topics that weekend were: "Low Budget on the Page," "Surviving Development," "Selling Your Script Without an Agent" and "Structure: Using It, Violating It."

The panels were composed predominantly of screenwriters, among them Nicholas Kazan (*Reversal of Fortune, Bicentennial Man*), Robin Swicord (*Little Women, Matilda*), Jon Favreau (*Swingers*), and Cauleen Smith (writer/director *Drylongso*). Joining the many writer panelists were producers, agents, studio execs, and entertainment attorneys. The conference offered case studies of two films.

The evolution of *Boys Don't Cry* was recounted by the film's co-writer/director, Kimberly Peirce, and its producer, Caroline Kaplan. The *American Beauty* case study was presented by the film's screenwriter, Alan Ball. Excerpts from Alan Ball's talk follow. [Note: The following took place after Alan Ball had won the Golden Globe and the Writers Guild Award, but prior to his picking up the Oscar for *American Beauty*.]

Alan: I was a playwright in New York, and I wrote a play, and got a job offer to come out and write for *Grace Under Fire*. And I figured okay, what the hell. I had never written a TV spec script, I didn't even watch TV.

But I was kind of sick of living in New York and I figured well, I should try this and see what happens. And I came out and I spent a season at *Grace Under Fire*, which was the second season of the show. And, you know, in a lot of ways it was the perfect first job to have because nothing will ever be that bad.

It was just hell at the beginning, and I really got sort of a slap in the face about—not in all TV shows, but in that show, particularly, how writers were just considered to be expendable and the script was kind of secondary to the persona of the star. And that was real new for me, because I had come out of the theater where writers have a certain amount of respect and control. And, you know, the flipside being that you can't make any money.

But my years in TV were invaluable to me because I have never taken a writing class. I studied acting in college. And I always had sort of an ear for dialog and sort of an instinct for character and in tone and mood, but writing for TV, producing an episode every week really seems to, I think, teach you the nuts and bolts of storytelling, which of course you kind of need to know.

And I left from *Grace Under Fire*; actually I was not invited back for the next season, and I was really upset for about ten minutes. And then I was offered a job on *Cybill*, which was the second season of that show. And both of those shows are shows that were really good the first season because they were driven by Chuck Lorre, who was the creator and the head writer, and then both of those shows went through a metamorphosis where the stars took creative control of the show. And in both cases I feel like those women really do the shows as P.R. for their lives. And it was a really volatile working environment. I spent three seasons on *Cybill* and I think we had a total of three executive producers, and she just goes through executive producers. And there were always big upheavals and half the staff would get fired, and those of us who stayed would get big promotions. In that way it was great, you know, because I was able to work my way up through the hierarchy quickly.

My last season on *Cybill*, I had just switched agencies because I really wanted a features career, and I had done some screenplays. I had done an adaptation of my play, *Five Women Wearing the Same Dress*, and I had done a rewrite for Warner Bros. And I really liked writing in that medium, but I felt like the agency where I was wasn't really that powerful in features and they kept saying, "Yeah, yeah, yeah, sure, we want you to have a features career," but really they just, you know, wanted to have my TV commission.

So I switched agencies and I went to UTA. And my features agent, Andrew Cannava, who, bless his heart, said, "Well, you need to write a new spec script because everybody has read these scripts of yours that are floating around town, they know what they are. I don't think I can get them set up anywhere, and I need something to reintroduce you to the features community because, frankly, nobody knows who you are."

And he was right. And so I said, "Well, can we meet somewhere and I'll pitch you some ideas I have." And I pitched him two fairly standard romantic comedies that were pretty, you know—if I couldn't pitch them in one sentence, I could pitch them in two. And then I pitched him *American Beauty*, which I had tried to write as a play years ago and I had sort of been toying around with these characters and their stories for years. And as you can imagine, the pitch was rambling, but I think I was really excited, you know.

"You think it's about this, but it's about something else, and you're feeling it—oh, and underneath it is all about this whole sort of what's the nature of reality and there's this kind of metaphysical thing." I was totally expecting him to just sort of go catatonic and fall out of his chair.

And to my surprise he says, "That's the one I think you should write." And I said, "Why?" And he said, "Because it's obviously the one you feel the most passionate about." It's the best piece of advice I ever got.

And so I started writing in June of '97, and I finished at the end of February of '98. I had been living with these characters and their stories for so long that I didn't—I don't like to write with an outline, or at least not a very concrete one because if I have to break the story into detail and write it out, then I sort of feel like I've written it, and I am so undisciplined that I never get around to writing the script.

For me part of the joy of writing is that sort of journey of discovery where surprises happen. And I finished it. It was 150 pages. I cut twenty-five out of it and I gave it to him. And he called me the next day and I was terrified because after four years of TV I was so used to saying, "Oh, okay. Here's my draft. Do whatever you want to do with it." But this was really personal and I had really invested myself in it the way I used to invest myself in the plays that I wrote, and I was terrified he was going to call and say, "Oh, my God, you're such a freak. I'll do us both a favor and just burn this."

And he said, "You know what, this is really good. With your permission what I'd like to do is just start talking it up." And he went around town to meetings and stuff and said, "This client of mine just gave me this screenplay that I think is really amazing."

And meanwhile, at the same time, he was putting together a very targeted list of producers he was going to give the screenplay to. Each of these producers had a specified territory. Dan Jinks and Bruce Cohen had DreamWorks and someone else had Paramount. And it was studios and independents.

Well, first of all, I never expected the script to sell. I thought I'd get some meetings out of it. And I thought if it did sell, it would end up at, you know, October, Artisan, or someplace like that.

Most of the studios passed, and those independents were the kind of places that seemed interested. And I had told Andrew, "I am not interested in selling this script to the highest bidder. If this movie gets made, it needs to get made in a very specific way and I think it needs to have not huge stars and it needs to retain the tone." And my big fear was that, first of all, that I'd be hired and rewritten; second of all, that somebody would come in and say, "Oh, it's so awful, does he have to die at the end, can't he learn his lesson, can't he get some therapy?" Or "It's so disgusting that he's hot for the teenage girl, can't she be a college student or maybe a woman at work?" Those kinds of notes that we always get all the time.

And so what he did is, whenever anybody made an offer he set up a meeting between me and these producers, and I just assumed that that was what always happened. It wasn't until later that I found out it wasn't. But I had gone to about four meetings and I had pretty much settled on one place, and he called me and he said, "Well, you need to wait because Steven Spielberg is reading the script tonight." And I thought well, that's a joke. He'll hate it. That was just total narrow-mindedness on my part, and much to my surprise he really liked it, and I went in and met at DreamWorks the next day, and they convinced me that it was the place to do it, and we sold it to DreamWorks.

And from that point on, I had sort of this charmed experience that I like to think was karmic payback for my years in the gulag of Cybill and Brett Butler.

There were a couple of big A-list directors that were very interested in doing it, and frankly, if they had been able to work it out schedule-wise, they would have gotten it. And one of them, his casting choices for Lester and Carolyn were Kurt Russell and Helen Hunt, which I heard and then wanted to bang my head against the wall.

Another one really wanted Ricky to rig Jane's house with those little lipstick-sized surveillance cameras and have her under constant surveillance. And I thought, oh, my God, he totally missed the point. But luckily both of those guys fell out and they gave it to Sam Mendes.

And Sam comes out of the theater as do I, and we usually spoke the same language, and we were sort of on the same page. I could tell that he really, really understood the script, he really got the tone, he really knew what it was about. And he wasn't threatened by me being around because he's used to working with writers.

His first choices for the lead roles were Kevin Spacey and Annette Bening, and they received offers and they both said yes. And then, you know, we got these amazing three kids and they all just sort of came together.

And Conrad Hall was going to do it, and Thomas Newman was going to do the score. And it had started out, DreamWorks had budgeted the movie at eight million. And then Kevin and Annette signed on—and both of them did the movie for much less than their usual fee. The budget went up to twelve and then we had a forty-day shooting schedule, which was very unrealistic, and we ended up shooting for fifty days.

And so the final budget was $15 million. And, at the time, DreamWorks was acting like we were the most financially irresponsible production in the history of time. But at the same time, they were focusing all their energy on

The Haunting and *Gladiator* which worked to our advantage because we sort of snuck in under the radar, and there was not a lot of studio interference.

And Sam is incredibly forceful, and he is one of the most brilliant men I've ever met, and he's also got that English accent so he's very intimidating. And I think, you know, sometimes DreamWorks' people would come up and say, "Well, what about this?" And he would just say, [English accent] "No! No! You can't do that. It doesn't make any sense!" And they'd go, "Oh . . ."

And then we wrapped the shoot and then several months later I went over to London to see his cut. In the original script there was a framing device of a big media trial at the beginning where Ricky and Jane are on trial because the videotape that you see has gotten its way into the hands of the police, actually the Colonel gave it to the police. And then "what is the movie now" unfolds and then at the end, interspersed between Lester's black-and-white memories of the moments of beauty in his life, you see the kids get convicted and go to jail.

Like I said, I was in a really angry state of mind when I was writing it because on *Cybill* we had what we called "a moment of shit" every week where somebody learns something—and usually from Cybill—and they hug and this sappy music comes on. You know, after three years of that, I would just cringe. And so when I got off on my own, it's like, "Yeah, the kids go to jail! Nothing means anything. Truth is irrelevant, ha!"

When I saw Sam's first cut all the stuff at the beginning had been cut and some of it had been left at the end, but not enough to make any sense. And I said, "What are you doing? You can't do that." And that was really the only time that we had words.

And then the next day he said, "I'd like to show you a cut where it's all been removed." And he did, and I realized well, you know, what, this movie turned out to be exactly what it's about. I thought it was one thing when I wrote it, and it was something entirely different. Beneath all the cynicism and the anger was this kind of lyrical heart, and I had to admit that—especially seeing the performances of Wes Bentley and Thora Birch as Ricky and Jane, to send them to jail for a crime they didn't commit was really cynical and kind of just awful, kind of nihilistic. And I realized I didn't want this movie to be nihilistic. I didn't want it to be about nothing. You know. And also I knew I could fight it, but I'd be outvoted. But I am not rationalizing it. Maybe I am rationalizing, but if I am I am unaware of it.

And then from that point on, DreamWorks' marketing got hold of it and did such an amazing job, and it became what it became. And I just sort of look at the whole thing and feel incredibly, incredibly grateful that such creative and gifted people came together to collaborate.

And also I am very, very aware of the big element of luck that is the thing that you have no control over, and so I feel like it's been the most rewarding experience of my life in terms of my life as a writer.

So that's sort of the framework of what happened.

At this point, I'll just open up the floor to questions.

Question: Sam Mendes is an amazing talent. Where does he come from?

Alan: He's a major director in the theater. He's won several Olivier Awards, which are the British equivalent to the Tonys, and he had directed his version of *Cabaret* originally at his theater in London, which is a very small theater, but it had moved to New York and had a huge hit on Broadway. And I actually saw it. I can't remember if it was before or after I met him, but I really liked it and I felt first of all, this was a man who knew how to get really good performances out of actors, and I knew the movie would rest on the strength of its performances.

He really understood humor from dark situations. He really understood how to create tableaus and use music and lighting to set a mood, and he also had a sense of rhythm. It didn't just barrel from point A to point B, there were ups and downs and swell moments, and moments with degrees and then huge surprising moments, and a real vital energy to it. So I was very impressed with his work.

And I also felt like he directed *Cabaret* in a way that was very creative, very unique, very much his own particular style, and yet it was always in service of the script. And I thought well, if he can bring that to this movie, then I am a very lucky man. And actually they had been offering him movies for years, but usually it had been costume dramas or British melodramas and that kind of thing. I think Steven Spielberg was a fan of his and was a fan of *Cabaret*, and I think they had met.

Question: What was in the twenty-five pages that you cut out, and what kind of a process did you use to cut it down to 125?

Alan: Because I started out as an actor so I play all these roles in my head when I'm writing and then I end up putting my own personal performance choices in as stage direction, and then I go back through and there will be a stage direction, "He sighs, and looks at his hand." I go through and cut all those out, because, you know, an actor is going to look at that and go "What?" And also on a page, it didn't make any sense because well, that could mean anything. So I'd just find ways to describe what was going on emotionally.

There was a big long sequence where Carolyn went to a radio station and recorded an ad and interacted with her secretary all before she goes to the sale house to try to sell it. There were a lot more scenes at the high school that were just basically repeating the same beats that are accomplished in that first scene, when Jane and Angela are at school.

A lot of it was just trimming descriptions and lines.

Question: I've seen a book, *American Beauty: The Shooting Script*. How is that different from the original script? And also, what kind of improv and changes happened as the shooting took place?

Alan: Right. The book that's published as the shooting script is actually the script of the movie as it turned out because they called me and they said, "That's what we want to do," and I said okay. It's different in that the framing device with the trial has been excised.

We had a two-week rehearsal period. Kevin and Annette both come out of theater as well, so it felt like old home week to me. We were sitting around and reading through the script and, you know, everybody had questions. They'd always have some questions, "What am I really saying here?" Usually you'd come up with an answer. If you don't have an answer but sometimes you just go, "You're—uh, well—" and then you'd make something up, and you realize you don't know so this part should probably change.

We did some improvisation, not a lot. The scene on the couch where she says, "Les, you're going to spill beer on the couch," grew out of that rehearsal period and out of some improv between Kevin and Annette.

A lot of it is stuff that Annette did because when Sam started out, he would throw out those very basic director questions, "Well, where were you right before this scene started?" And everybody would go, "Hmmm. Let's see." And Annette just without missing a beat would go, "Well, I was at the dry cleaners and not only did they ruin my blouse, but somebody nicked my car. And they've ruined more than one blouse, and I am considering taking legal action because, if you have nice things, you should be able to take care of them." And she just started channeling this woman. And we were all kind of going, "Whoa." I mean this is on Day One, okay. And she is nothing like that in real life. She is the absolute opposite and so my personal theory is that she was channeling her mother.

And then there was a scene where Jane and Angela gave Ricky a ride home and they were on a highway, and there was a car wreck, and Ricky filmed it, and then they ended up at home, and that would have taken three days to do. We would have had to close off the Interstate and we were running over and they came to me and said, "Can you cut this scene?" And I said, "No." Because there was a line in that scene that beats the heart and soul of this movie so you can't cut it. And they said, "Well, can we figure out a way to shoot it that will be a lot cheaper?" And that's when the decision was made for at the schoolyard for Jane to decide to walk home with him, and then they would just walk home. And that saved the scene, and we were also able to shoot all of that in one day and save a lot of money.

In the masturbation scene Sam told Kevin just to make up different euphemisms every time the camera started rolling so he would, you know, freak Annette out more.

I was on the set every day except two, and mostly I just sat over in the corner and stared at the monitor and laughed. Everything was going so great. I spent about the first month rushing up to Kevin and Annette going, "Oh, my God, you're so great. You're so great." And Kevin would just go, "Hmmm, okay, thanks." But then I calmed down.

Then I spent a lot of time watching the way Sam and Connie [Conrad Hall] were setting up the shots and watching the way Sam worked with the actors because that's why I wanted to be on the set, I have aspirations to direct myself, but I've never been involved in shooting a movie, and I didn't feel confident to try to do that because my only experience has been on stage and in television, and the format of television is very, very different. So I wanted to kind of soak up the experience as much as I could. And everybody was really gracious, you know.

They made me a promise at the very beginning, Dan and Bruce, because I said in our first meeting "I want to be a part of this and I want you to keep me informed of everything that's going on along the way," and they said, "We promise you." You know what, they kept that promise, and I'll always be indebted to them.

Although Sam later said, "You know, if we hadn't gotten along so well and if you, had been what I consider to be trouble, I would have barred you from the set." And I am sure he would have.

Question: Could you talk a little bit about that journey from finishing your script to Oscar nomination—how it's affected you? Does it seem kind of surrealistic to you?
Alan: Oh, it's totally surreal. It's completely surreal. The two days that I was not on the set I was pitching an idea for a pilot, one at NBC and one at ABC, because I had signed a three-year television development deal a week before *American Beauty* sold. And I had cashed all their checks so. . . . As much as I thought, oh, now I am a movie writer—oh, now I am supposed to do this, aren't I?

I went in to pitch, you know, the first idea that popped in my head, which is sort of for a period of seven years when I lived in New York, I lived in Brooklyn in a brownstone with three other guys and a dog. And it was a mixture of gay men and straight men, and it was just not an issue. And so I just went in and pitched that and then I added an ex-wife and a teenage daughter, you know, thinking well, maybe somebody will like this, but more than likely they're going to say, "We've got this really obscure insane comedian that we'd love for you to build a show around." But they didn't, and they liked it, and then the next thing I knew I was writing a pilot, and the next thing I knew we were shooting it [*Oh, Grow Up* on ABC], and then the next thing I knew it on the schedule. So right after the movie wrapped, I went into that. And so Dan and Bruce would call me and say well, this is happening and this is happening, and I'd go, that's interesting, but I got to go to a run-through in five minutes.

But there was an article that appeared in the *New York Times* that sort of said "Oh, forget about the summer movies, this movie is the next big thing." And there was ain't-it-cool-news, which I had never been aware of, but there was a big thing about the movie on that. They started to show Sam's cut to critics and they kept calling and saying, "This is really big." Running a network TV show is—it becomes your life. So I would sort of go, oh, that's really good, I have to go to casting now.

And actually when the show premiered at the Toronto Film Festival, I went to the network run-through on Friday, came back, did half the rewrite, left my instructions with the staff, got in the car, went to the airport, took the red eye, showed up in Toronto, did four hours of press junkets. That's when I knew that people were treating this as if it was something kind of out of the ordinary.

Went to the screening that night, went to this big party after the screening, went back to the hotel, crashed. The next day got on a plane and flew back here, and we started shooting that week's episode on Monday.

So it was weird because it was going on but at the same time I had this other thing that really was more than a full-time job. And so I wasn't really aware of it.

They would fax me the really good reviews because I said I didn't want to see the bad ones. And then I went to some screenings and then I went to a screening in Los Feliz at The Vista. And it was two or three weeks after it had opened wide, and that was really fun because I really got to see—because I had only seen it with industry audiences, and that was really fun because I got to see what just a more regular audience thought of it. And they were really rowdy and, you know, really liked a lot of the darker—really much more willing to laugh at a lot of the darker comedy, which I was pleased. Because sometimes the industry audiences are like, "Oh, this is very important"—at things that I always thought were hysterical, you know. So when the other audiences did too I was sort of vindicated.

And then my show got cancelled and it was kind of an awful experience because I had gotten really attached to the writing staff and the cast. I mean, it becomes your life and your family and then all of a sudden it gets cancelled. And the reason it was cancelled was because they wanted to run a game show three hours a week, which was kind of hard to take.

So I was really upset, and I went home, and my mom had fallen down the stairs and broken her collar bone and life just suddenly got really weird and bizarre, and I started smoking again. And then all of a sudden, the movie started getting all these nominations and I did too, and that sort of helped me.

Question: I guess you believe in the script now and you think it's okay?
Alan: Yeah. Sam said something very interesting, I had lunch with him

yesterday, and he said something very interesting. He said, "When you came to London and you saw the cut, you know, your reaction really wasn't 'How dare you do that to my work,' it was 'Oh, my God, I did a bad job with that framing device, it wasn't good. I failed somehow.'" I'm my own worst critic and then, of course, all the accolades and especially all the award stuff and going to those shows is—I am so cynical about it because for years I would sit at home drinking, screaming at the TV, and now I am there, and it's weird. It's very exciting, you know. It is so disconnected from the work. It's really seductive. I can see why so many celebrities go crazy.

Question: So it is fun?
Alan: It is fun. Yeah. Yeah. As long as there is liquor at the table.

Question: After having this great feature experience and after kind of book-ending it with your sitcom experience and most importantly being the head of your own show, how do you feel about on Monday, it's really a funny joke, but on Friday it isn't?—but whereas the same joke still is alive and wonderful for a year in *American Beauty*.
Alan: Well, that's because you don't do six run-throughs of a scene before you shoot it. The actors rehearsed, but good film actors really hold back until they get in front of a camera to try to let something spontaneous happen.

Whereas, in a sitcom, you know, the joke can kill at table, it's still funny at the run-through the next day, and then on Wednesday, everybody's heard it. So that's just part of the nature of sitcom writing is you realize some really funny jokes are going to just fall out, because you have to keep the network people and the studio people laughing.

And what's amazing is that they don't realize this, but I would always just in the back of my mind, I'd go that's a really good joke, it just sort of laid there like a dead smelly thing in today's run-through, so let's rewrite it, but when we got in front of the audience on the second take, I would always say go back to my other joke just for the tag, and whichever one the audience responded to more is the one we would put in.

Question: It's such an interesting mixture of tone, in the writing process did you have to work with that a lot so that it felt natural to the story?
Alan: I think that mixture in tone is sort of the way I look at the world. I go through days where it's just incredibly hysterical, absurd things happen and then, you know, something ridiculous will make me cry for thirty seconds. And so I never thought, "I am going to set out and try to mix all these different tones." It just sort of happened, and it wasn't conscious.

I knew I wanted it to be funny because when I go see movies and there's not a single ounce of humor in them, I just want to put a bullet in my brain, you know. But I knew I wanted it to be about something and to have more depth than your standard sitcom episode, where because of the nature of it you have to get the punch lines, you have twenty-two minutes, you've got the network basically giving you the same two notes over and over and over again. "Make everybody nicer" and "Articulate the subtext." I think they are really just so diametrically opposed to really good dramatic writing.

So I wanted it to be about something, to have some meaning and depth and about characters who were searching for meaning in their lives as opposed characters with expensive clothing who were just trading insults.

Question: Before you sent it out to your agent, did you show it to a lot of your friends and peers?
Alan: I showed it to two friends.

In my first draft, Lester sleeps with Angela, but I never intended it to be like he goes, "Oh, my God, I'm going to score with a teenage girl." It goes up to the same point it is in the movie and then once she reveals that she's a virgin, he hesitates, she says, "No, no. I want to do this." And then it becomes about they drop their masks and then it becomes about making love, but to capture that would have been so subtle and so elusive, because I don't think anybody would have seen beyond the actual sex.

And I struggled with that because I got that note from the studio and I thought, oh, they just want to make it "nicer." Then I realized, no, no, no. He becomes a father to her that he can't be with his own daughter, and then I was able to realize that it's a much better choice anyway.

But in my very first draft that happened, and both my friends said, "You might want to consider having him not sleep with her." And I was still in my bitter angry, "I've just enjoyed three years of Cybill Shepherd" state of mind. So I said, "No. No. He has to. You're a puritan. You're a stinking puritan. If you were European, this wouldn't matter." And I was wrong, it was a really wrong choice.

Question: The closing monologue, how was it written and when was it written? My sense of it was—I loved the movie—but there was kind of a smugness of him that I didn't understand following what we'd seen him just go through with her.

And I don't know if "smugness" is really the right word, but there was something transformative about him—in that scene where he does not sleep—and he looks at the photo of the family. And we kind of return to—kind of an old sound for him, and I just want you to talk about that. Maybe I missed it.
Alan: Well, the closing monologue is in the first draft. At the time it was interspersed with scenes of the kids taking the rap and going to jail, and the Colonel like alone in his room crying and his wife discovering this bloody shirt, and Carolyn being with Buddy, but not being able to sleep and things like that.

His tone is the same tone that's at the beginning of the movie, because he's narrating from beyond. He's narrating from the point of being dead. I never found it smug.

I know it's kind of weird, but he is in the same place—in the voiceovers, he's always in the same place because he's already experienced it. We as an audience haven't, but he has.

What he learned is, you know, you can't hold onto anything. You can't own anything ultimately. And life passes through you and—

Question: I think it's just the line: "shitty little life."
Alan: Oh, "A stupid little life"?

Question: Yeah. There's something about that that seems—anyway, I loved the movie. I loved it. It's just there's something about that that's made me think. I didn't have the experience he wanted me to have, because the life that we ended up seeing was beautiful.
Alan: I think he's saying that when he says, "I can't feel anything but gratitude for every single moment of my stupid little life."

Question: Yeah.
Alan: He's saying it with great kindness.

Question: Good.
Alan: He's saying it with amusement. I mean the subtext was that my life on some level was insignificant and these choices I made were ridiculous. I mean, I lusted after this teenage girl, and I became this pot smoking, you know, gym rat. That's stupid. But that experience was something that I would never trade for anything because I was alive.

Question: Did the title evolve or was that—
Alan: No. It was always there.

Question: You spoke earlier of replacing stage directions with some other way to get a point across. How do you do that?
Alan: It's, you know, "He pulls out the empty bag of pot, he's not happy about it." You just put something very generic, "He's not happy about it" so that an actor can then figure out whatever way they want to express that, or something that's a little more specific.

I feel like a lot of times the first draft of the script is not a shooting script. It's a presentation. It's a presentation for studio people. And a lot of studio people need to be spoon fed because they aren't creative. And so I write it for them. I tend to break a lot of rules apparently. I didn't realize that, but if I have a very specific line reading in mind, I'll boldface and italicize the words so it jumps off the page, and then before you get to the actors, you take all that out. But, you know, that person who is doing the coverage on the movie you got to give them a little extra.

I mean there are people who do coverage who are incredibly brilliant and who will move their way up the ranks; there are also people who, you know, are just dull and not creative, and they more than likely will move up through the ranks before the really creative person. So I tend to go a little overboard with that.

Question: You don't necessarily work in an outline, but I am wondering what—do you have some sort of broad strokes in mind or maybe—
Alan: Yeah. I knew Lester died. I knew it would look like Jane and Ricky killed him, I knew I wanted you to start the movie thinking they killed him, I wanted halfway through the movie you to go, no, it's not them, oh, my God, it's the wife. And then to be surprised that it was the Colonel. But then as I wrote it, it became less about the plot and more about what each person was kind of experiencing because they all go through a sort of transformation or they come to a point where they can go through some sort of transformation.

The Colonel and Carolyn, of course, can't because they can't let go of the need to control their lives and try to be someone that they're not because they think that that will make them happy. And to me they're the two most tragic characters in the movie.

Question: The dancing bag, was that written?
Alan: Uh-huh. Yeah. That happened to me ten years ago. I was walking home from brunch and a plastic bag came out of nowhere and sort of circled me about—literally about twenty-five times. And, you know, it was a weird un-expected profound moment and I always felt like I was in the presence of something; that always stuck with me. I hadn't planned to put it in the movie, but then Ricky said, "You want to see the most beautiful thing I ever filmed," and I thought well, shit, what is that going to be? And then I felt well, what is the most the beautiful thing I ever saw or the most beautiful moment I ever experienced and it was that so I put it in fully thinking that nobody would understand it, and that they would want to change it. Apparently it's become most people's favorite part.

Question: Is that the "American Beauty" that you're referring to or is it more sarcastic?
Alan: No. The first perception of it is the rose, American Beauty rose, that's a specific breed of rose. Then "American Beauty" refers to Angela. You know, she's the American beauty, she's blonde, cheerleader, blue eyes, sort of an

archetype of an American dreamgirl. But really "American Beauty" is that plastic bag, okay.

Question: Would you talk about starting the movie with a guy that says "I'm dead." I remember *Sunset Boulevard* started that way. I was thinking, is this to ease the fact that the guy died so you don't feel so bad, since he's talking, he must be in heaven? What's your theory?

Alan: You know what, I am not aware of what the theory is. I don't think that way. It's more organic. That's just sort of what came out and it felt right.

I am one of those writers for whom the actual writing process itself teaches me what I think and believe as opposed to the other way around. So now I am being forced to articulate what that means.

I think there is some sort of life after death. He's narrating from beyond the grave. I knew it was important to know. A lot of the movie is about living with mortality and living with death and the notion—not the notion, the fact that, you know, it's something we'll all face, but we live in a culture that really wants to hide it and cover it up and pretend it doesn't exist.

And so I guess it was important to know that he was going to die, but then you sort of forget it. Because he says it at the beginning and then when all the trial stuff was taken out, he just sort of says it once and then you're going on with the story. And you think "Oh, my God, I just saw that video, the kids are going to kill him." But then you get caught up in the story and you sort of forget it.

Question: Ordinarily you don't want the audience to know how a story is going to end. You go to great pains to conceal how it's going to end.

Alan: It wasn't a conscious choice. My process is really kind of weird and organic in a way that sometimes works and sometimes it's just a big mess. But I don't think about what things mean. I didn't think about what that red door meant, I just knew it had to be red. And then I hear Sam talk about it in interviews and explain what it is, and I am like, "Oh, yeah!"

Question: In the original draft at the beginning you have Lester flying around like Superman. Whose idea was it to take that out? And also, who or what inspired Ricky Fitts?

Alan: It was Sam's idea to take that out. Again, we shot all that. We shot all the trial footage and we shot the flying—when Lester had the dream of flying before he wakes up when the alarm clock goes off, and Sam felt that it just sort of looked too—well, it was a combination of being a little too clever and not really looking good. It looked kind of cheap, you know, because we didn't really have the money to afford the kind of effects that we really needed to make that work.

So that was mostly his choice, and I agreed with it. I fought more about the trial stuff, but when I saw flying stuff I figured, yeah, it looks kind of cheap.

And what inspired Ricky Fitts? Well, the moment I had with the plastic bag certainly inspired him. I grew up in a household that was not entirely dissimilar from Ricky Fitts's home. And the character of Carolyn—when she starts slapping herself after she can't sell the house. I hadn't planned that. But all of a sudden I was typing it, and I was like—she's so unhappy, she's so deeply, deeply unhappy.

I know a lot of people think she's very cartoonish. But I certainly have known women like that, and men like that, but I find her so sad. So very sad, because she just has bought the entire pack of lies and she's thinking it will make her happy.

Question: How much did the movie change from the script?
Alan: I think the notion of writing a script that is complete and then you just shoot it exactly as written, I don't think so much happens, it's such a collaborative process—and I also think movies and any sort of collaborative venture, it takes on a life of its own at some point, and you have to be able to recognize that and step back, and I think you have to be willing to make changes along the way. And I think a lot of writing gets done in the editing room too.

When Sam was cutting the movie, he said, in trying to convince me to lose the trial sequence. "Look, it's like the movie is letting us know what it wants to be." And he was right.

Question: The scene where Annette Bening hugs the clothes at the end, I love that scene—was that Annette or was that you?
Alan: That was Annette. That was her idea. During rehearsals she said, "I feel like, I don't know, I feel like I should have a moment when I open the closet and smell him on his clothes and just hug it and cry." And I went, "All right. That's good. I'll add it to the script, you know. Yeah. I think that's a great idea so I'll go write it."

Question: Did I misunderstand you? It sounds like you sat down, wrote 150 pages, went back in took out twenty-five pages of "looks at his hand and sighs," handed it in, got it sold, and got awards? I mean, wasn't there any agonizing over—
Alan: Well, you've got to remember, I tried writing this as a play eight years ago. I've been living with these characters for eight years. And of course, when I cut twenty-five pages out of it, I went to Laguna and checked into a hotel and I was there for three days because it's hard—you know.

Question: But didn't you agonize over well, let's see, would this scene work, would that scene work, or did it really kind of flow very easily for you?

Alan: Well, I—it flowed very easily for me, and I am also a writer who if I am on page thirty and something new occurs to me that I know I have to go back to page fifteen and put something in so it will make sense, I do it right then, you know, and then I keep going.

After the script sold, we made a decision for Lester to not sleep with Angela, we also cut this flashback to Vietnam that the Colonel had, where he had like a romantic sexual experience with another soldier in a tent, and they were ambushed, and the guy got killed in front of him and died in his arms, and he found out that the guy's name was Rick. Because it totally tips the scene in the garage. I just needed to write that scene so I knew what his back story was. If he felt like he had to deny who he was because God would punish him, it's irrational. And so those were big changes, taking those out. And then I worked with Sam on the script for a while before it went out to actors. Sam would call me like every two weeks and go, "Why don't you come over and we'll just go through the script."

He actually had me read the script to him because he wanted to hear my inflections reading those characters for him. And I have since found out that that is something he always does.

And then we had the two-week rehearsal period and we continued to make changes and it took me eight months to write this script. It wasn't like I just sat down and it came out in one week. It was hard, but it was really exciting. But, yeah, it was kind of a really unbelievably easy ride in terms of what usually happens.

Just remember that I had to go into Cybill Shepherd and just sit there while she went, "I have a bad haircut, I think we should do this week's episode about my hair." You know, "and I think I should eat something and stuff it into my face. That's funny." So there was misery, it was just elsewhere.

Question: You say you wanted to direct—a small indie film or a studio film?
Alan: I have a year and half of my TV deal, and, you know, I have continued to cash their checks so what I did is when I went home for Christmas I wrote a spec pilot for HBO, and they're trying to pan out a deal, and if they do, then I'll direct that. I am also writing a spec feature because basically everything that I've taken a meeting on, they're too high profile, they're too high budget, and there are too many people with ideas about what they want to make it. And nothing really struck me.

But there is one idea that an actor brought me who has some clout, and it's a really good idea. And he basically said, "All I have is a starting place, why don't you just go with this. If I can get the studio to bankroll it, would you be interested?" I said sure.

So that's what I am doing right now. I am going to direct a pilot, and the spec that I am writing I hope to direct.

Question: So you don't really mind going back and forth between TV and features and whatever?

Alan: Well, I kind of have to. You know what I do like about TV is the social aspect of it, of going into a room and being with other creative people and laughing and having fun. I don't like spending, you know, all day alone. I like it sometimes.

Question: How much of you is in Lester and these other characters?

Alan: There's a lot of me in Lester and a lot of me in Ricky. There was a lot of me in Lester hating his job, you know, having to run *Cybill*. There's a lot of Cybill in Carolyn. There's a lot of me in Ricky, there's a lot of my dad in the Colonel, and there's a lot of my mom in the Colonel's wife. There's a lot of girls I knew in high school and college in Jane, and there's a lot of various people in the industry in Buddy, King of Real Estate.

Two very dear friends of mine from earlier in my life, one of whom is no longer with us, are the gay couple. But I don't sit down and go, "Well, this is obviously Cybill." People would say, "Who is that character?" And I thought, you know, she has this mythology about herself in her life that is totally false and yet she pours every kind of energy into maintaining it, and in the process she's kind of deeply lost and really isolated and unhappy.

I identify very much with Lester. The rest of them are just bits and pieces of me. I mean there's a part of me in all of them because I think you have to identify with the character at some point when you're writing them, otherwise they're just going to become—I mean you don't have to identify with them personally, but you have to identify with them as a human being and be able to see through their eyes otherwise they'll just become puppet-like, you know what I mean?

But the Colonel, a lot of people say, "Oh, he's so evil." And I so didn't see that, it was just that he was so shattered and so broken and so deeply, deeply, deeply alone.

Question: I would like to know what you liked best and what you liked least about your script.

Alan: There are a couple of lines I really liked. I really liked the scene where it shows you the plastic bag. There's that whole day after Lester starts buying pot where all their lives take off and change, and I really love the way that moves between Lester's story and Angela's story and Carolyn's story, and it's really funny and really sad and kind of goes back and forth between tones in a way.

What I like least, I wish I could rewrite the garage scene. There are a couple of lines that are sort of double entendre-ish between Lester and Colonel that now when I see it, I sort of feel like I wish I had been less—I wish he was a little more open, but did he have to say, "Our marriage is just for show,

"Please get out of those clothes," and things like that that the Colonel could misinterpret.

I've seen the movie so many times now that I am seeing all the weird little continuity glitches and things drive me crazy like the fact that she looks through the garage and sees him smoking pot, and then automatically she's opening the garage with the remote. What? Does she just carry it around with her?

For the most part I am pretty proud of it. I feel like it's probably the best work I've ever done.

Question: You said you started as an actor. How did that help you as a writer?
Alan: I think it makes it easier to write for actors. I think if you've spent some time on stage and you've spent some time saying dialog, and that's all I did in college and for many years after that I tried to make a go of it as an actor. And I started writing to give myself things to do because nobody was casting me.

I think if you know what it is to be an actor, you're quicker to recognize, man, that would be a hard line to say, you know. And if you're just sort of acting the role in your head as you write it, then it tends to have a flow to it. And I think you learn how to write for actors.

Question: I know a writer who has written like twenty fiction books, and he'll be in the middle of a cocktail conversation and he'll hear a good line, take out a notecard, and write it down. Do you do that?
Alan: I don't write them down, but it's in my head. I mean I was at a U2 concert, and this girl was standing on a chair in front of me, and she goes, "Oh, my God, I love you, I want to have ten thousand of your babies!" And I just thought oh, my God. And then I remembered it and put it in Angela's line.

Question: Was it Sam's idea to cast Kevin Spacey?
Alan: Uh-huh.

Question: You must have been so pleased?
Alan: Yeah. I don't think of actors when I write because the characters seem real enough, but when Sam said, "Well, I think, you know, we should try to get Kevin Spacey and Annette Bening." And I said, "Yeah. That's good."

Question: Not only because he's a wonderful actor, but also because you have similar speech patterns.
Alan: I know. People have told me that. Actually the first day I drove onto the set, the security said, "Oh, Mr. Spacey, your trailer is right over there" and I said, "Well, I am not Kevin Spacey. I'm the writer." He said, "Oh, well, you need to park way over there."

People that know me have said, "It's like Kevin is doing you." I don't think that, I just think that, you know, there are similarities. But now I can't imagine anyone else playing him. He was born to play that.

Question: Does it make you want to do more one-camera stuff?
Alan: Yeah. I am going to stay away from four camera stuff for a while.
First of all, the landscape right now is incredibly hostile to sitcoms. Everybody—the media— has decided that they're dead. And also the networks, you know, they're just dying. I mean the fact that we got on the air is amazing. You really have very little chance of getting on the air unless you're actually producing it through the network and they have a huge portion of the back-end. There's so many weird politics.

I mean in our case, once they decided they wanted *Who Wants to Be a Millionaire?* three hours a week, they only had room for one half-hour time slot, and that went to *Sports Night*—which is the Disney Channel. *Sports Night* is a great show. I am not saying that we should have gotten it, but it's just—that's—the nature is so awful—it's so hard to do it, and I am very, very fortunate I know because I spent four years in it and have a level of financial security, that I don't have to scramble to figure out, you know, where the next paycheck is going to come from. But I feel like HBO is really a place to go. That's the future of TV.

Question: Is that part about government-grown marijuana real?
Alan: You know what, somebody told me about that and I didn't know if it was actually true or not, but I just put it in the script, you know, because it sounded so great. And we were sitting at the table, we were sitting around the table during rehearsal, and somebody said, "Is that real?—that whole thing about the marijuana?"—and I was prepared to make up my story, you know, because I have no idea, but Wes Bentley just went, "Uh, yeah."

Question: I wanted to ask you about the roses, which I loved. Where in your creative process did that come about and was it always an identifying device or did that come gradually?
Alan: That was in the first draft, all the roses imagery. I am not sure where it came from. It and the title came at sort of the same time. And, again, I think it's a symbol. At the time I was writing, I didn't know what it was a symbol of except that I saw it and I saw the opening of the shirt and roses coming out.

The first draft, she wasn't on the ceiling, she was sort of floating in this swirl of roses and they were raining down and that would have cost so much to do that—and, again, that was "Can we make it cheaper?" and it ended up being much better.

Because Sam's whole notion for the fantasy sequence was a very concrete visual style, there's not a lot of morphing weirdness we're used to from, you know, fantasy sequences, which I think is what makes them so striking.

But I guess the roses and the color red are symbolic of passion and being passionate and being alive. But at the time I just knew that that's what I saw. He's experiencing sort of a second blooming, which he foolishly thinks is about becoming an adolescent again but it's really just about rediscovering the passion for living that he had at that time in his life that he had forgotten, and that so many people forget, you know.

Question: When you were going to Laguna Beach to do your rewrite, did you closet yourself alone for three days and write until you dropped at the computer, or did you get up and go to the beach and run around and then come back and write?
Alan: I am sure you are all used to, you know, sitting at a computer and then all of a sudden, "Oh, isn't it time I should clean out the fridge?" So I got out of my house so I wouldn't be able to do any of that.

I would go to the beach and go swimming and stuff like that, but mostly I just forced myself to do it. I knew I had to do it. And I said, you know, I have to do this before I go home. I had a weekend to do it, so . . .

Question: Was that difficult?
Alan: Well, like I said, I had been living with the characters for eight years. There was a certain flow to the writing process that was really nice, a nice experience. But the first draft was structurally very sound. We made the decision for him not to sleep with Angela, we made the decision for the Colonel not to have that flashback to Vietnam, and in editing certain things were moved around. I think in the first draft the sequence at the high school takes place before Carolyn tries to sell the house. It just worked better.

Question: So you cut twenty-five pages before the producers read it?
Alan: I was just trying to get it down to 125, to make sure that every word was exactly perfect. You know that whole thing. And the minute you make copies, you immediately—the first page you open to, you see a huge glaring typo.

Question: During the eight months where you were writing, could you describe some of what your work was like, I mean were you writing from "Fade in" to "Fade out" or would you dabble around at it?
Alan: Well, my daily work was running *Cybill* because the executive producer had left to run the Damon Wayans show, and so I was running a show, and then at night, you know, everybody would go, "Let's go to Mexicali and have margaritas," and I would say, "No. I am going to go home and go work on my screenplay."

And I was literally surviving on no sleep and—but it was so much fun to actually go home and write something I gave a shit about. I mean I did my job seriously, and I never sloughed off, but, you know, you get a note like, "Well, I want Billy's boyfriend to fall in love with me, and I want to sing opera." And all you can do is go, "Okay." And then you go off to your room, and you're going well, I don't know how to make this work without it looking incredibly egotistical and narcissistic, but we got to try.

Ultimately you don't have that level of organic connection because you can't, because if you did you'd go crazy. It would be too painful. And plus, you know, they were characters that were set in the first season of the show. They weren't my characters, it wasn't my voice, I was a craftsman. I knew Cybill's voice, I knew Christine's voice and I knew what would make a good scene and everything.

But I thought, this is shit. This is really a stupid idea, but, you know, I had to do it. And so it was really liberating to go home even at one o'clock in the morning and go, "Yeah, she's in a bathtub full of roses," and sort of lose myself in it.

Question: Did you guys want an unknown for Angela?
Alan: I wanted unknowns for all of the kids. We saw every teenage actor in town. And a lot of them are quite good, but I felt like if the kids were unfamiliar faces, that you would really get to know them as a character; whereas if you have *Buffy, the Vampire Slayer* and any of those walking in, it would feel—I mean we saw Christina Ricci and she was great for Jane, but I felt like I've seen her do that and the minute she comes on screen, you know who she is. And she's played that role before and I thought it would be more interesting if they were three faces that we didn't really know. And luckily Sam agreed.

Question: Is it because you're a dynamite writer that you had control or is it because you had *Cybill* or luck? How did you manage the position where you pretty much were in charge of your script?
Alan: I think the keyword is luck. I think the script spoke to the producers and the director and the people involved in a way that they wanted to retain me and my voice, they were interested in having me around. You know, but again, that's incredibly lucky.

Question: It also sounds like the answer is to write a great script.
Alan: Well, thank you, but I think there are probably a lot of instances where really great scripts, the writers have been hired and rewritten, and it becomes something not as good. I think it was a combination of the right people got the script and luck and the fact that DreamWorks was busy producing *Gladiator.*

Question: Are you still tempted to write parts for yourself as an actor?

Alan: No. I've given that up. Over the years it's become really clear to me that my strength as a writer far outweighed my strength as an actor. It was fun acting, I loved it.

Question: And what was your parents' response to the film?

Alan: My father is dead. My mother read it and she said, "That's the filthiest thing I've. . . ." But now she's very, very happy. She's really. . . . Oh, my God, getting nominated for awards has validated me with my family and I am very happy about that. For years I was the freak, you know.

Question: Did she recognize her relationship with your father in it?

Alan: If she did, she didn't say anything. I was nervous about her seeing it. I didn't see her with it, but I was nervous about the point where Ricky kisses her on the cheek and says, "I wish things had been better for you." That's something that I've always, always felt and it always makes me cry in the movie because of my own personal connection to it. And I think if I were to watch the movie with her, it would be incredibly uncomfortable.

Question: Did you ever think about winning an Oscar?

Alan: When I was a kid I thought, oh, I am going to be a big movie star someday, I am going to win an Oscar. And then I sort of developed this viewpoint of like this outsider who was totally cynical. And that's when I would watch the awards shows and just scream at the TV. "Shut up!" "Get off!" You know. And that's actually the way I watched the awards last year. So it should be surreal.

Question: I noticed on Lester's desk it says "Look Closer." I am guessing the advertising came from that.

Alan: But that was the set dresser, that wasn't in the script. The set dresser just put that in his cubicle. And Sam watching footage day-in and day-out during editing, he saw that; and there was that great shot where—you know, there are two shots—there's one of Lester reflected in the screen of the computer, and then there's a wide shot showing all the cubicles, and then there's that one that's sort of moving in very slowly, very fluid, and you see that "Look Closer."

He was very, very hands-on in putting together the trailer, and the poster. He fought for a poster that did not feature those packaged faces. His instincts are pretty dead on. I feel like I've been very lucky to work with him, and I'll jump at the chance to work with him again.

Question: You think when it comes out on DVD, they'll show the scenes that were cut from the trial?

Alan: No. He feels like the movie is the movie and he doesn't want to do anything to change that. But there is a track on the DVD with him and me, and he basically talks and I am just saying, "Oh, cool. You're so great. You're so great."

Question: If you hadn't had Sam and would have directed it yourself, what do you think might have happened as an end result of the film?
Alan: Well, I think it would have been much worse. Yeah. I think I—well, I mean, I just wasn't ready. I can't even imagine that. It would be such a learning experience and I wouldn't want to do that to the script.

Question: When you do your first feature, where will you look for that second pair of eyes without Sam?
Alan: The cinema photographer and the producers. Yeah. I mean whoever the first AD is, you know. I am very glad—and I am very aware having worked in TV for so many years that other people can have other ideas and a lot of the time, they're going to be better than mine, and it's just going to make it work better and that's what's really important.

Also, I feel like as a writer you have a very specific vision when you're writing a piece, but the main purpose of that vision is to get the piece on paper. And once it's there, it's going to become a collaborative thing, and other people are going to bring stuff to it that improves it. You know, if you want to retain total control, then you should write novels. And even then, you know, editors are going to mess with it.

But I know being a writer in this town is incredibly frustrating and you have to deal with a lot of pinheads and morons, but there are a lot of people out there who are smart and who are very good in this. If you're lucky enough to be working with good people, they're going to improve the work.

And something happens when it goes from the page to the screen, you know, like we were talking about earlier, like the trial stuff I thought worked on the page and it totally didn't work on screen. You have to be open, you have to be able to recognize when, as Sam said, the movie is letting you know what it wants to become, and you just get out of its way.

Gaywatch: Alan Ball Goes *Six Feet Under*

CHRISTINE CHAMPAGNE / 2001

From *Planet Out*, Gay.com Network, 2001. Reprinted by permission of Christine Champagne.

Alan Ball, the openly gay Oscar-winning writer of the 1999 film *American Beauty*, brings his talents to television as the creator of HBO's new series *Six Feet Under*. Actually, Ball is hardly a stranger to television. He spent years as a producer and writer on diva-driven sitcoms like *Grace Under Fire*, starring Brett Butler, and Cybill Shepherd's *Cybill*, and he created *Oh, Grow Up*, a 1999 sitcom that featured a prominent gay character.

Six Feet Under also includes a gay character, the decidedly uptight and in-the-closet David Fisher (played by Michael C. Hall, whose credits include the Broadway show *Cabaret*).

For those of you who haven't checked out the show yet, David works at Fisher & Sons Funeral Home in Los Angeles. After family patriarch Nathaniel Fisher (Richard Jenkins) is killed in a car accident, the Fisher family, which includes David's free-spirited brother Nate (*Sports Night* alum Peter Krause), tortured mom Ruth (Frances Conroy, nominated for a Tony for her role in *The Ride Down Mt. Morgan*) and wild sister Claire (Lauren Ambrose) must deal with death head on and carry on the family business.

Six Feet Under is dramatic, but it is also darkly funny. Gaywatch recently dug up some inside scoop on the show—including some tidbits on David's future exploits—when I spoke with Ball.

Champagne: I have to admit that I was a little nervous about tuning into *Six Feet Under* because I thought the show might be morbid. I was relieved to see that you injected so much humor into the show.

Ball: I wanted the tone of the show to be playful because it is such a potentially upsetting subject. I wanted to establish right from the get-go that we weren't going to wallow in the morbidity.

Champagne: Were at all familiar with the funeral industry before you began writing the pilot?

Ball: I had been to funerals, and they had been fairly traumatic and surreal experiences. So I had a certain feel about funeral homes and what they do. But no, I wasn't familiar with the industry. I did a lot of reading. I went all over the Web. You'd be surprised at the stuff that's on the Web. You can actually arrange your entire funeral on the Web. I studied some textbooks from mortuary schools. But I never went and witnessed an embalming or anything like that. I didn't feel that was necessary, and frankly, I didn't want to do it.

Champagne: Some writers tell me they purposely set out to include gay characters in their projects. Others say the characters just spring up. How did you come to include a gay character on your show?

Ball: Well, as a writer, I'm very instinctive. I usually don't map things out or plan things. I just sort of follow my instincts, and David was always gay from the very beginning—somebody who has such a good boy complex and is trying to do the right thing and make everybody happy except himself. It's such a classic gay thing.

Champagne: I have to say that I found it refreshing that he was in the closet. Everyone is so out and proud on TV these days, and that's not how everyone lives.

Ball: They're out and proud and well adjusted, and they never have sex. [He laughs.]

Champagne: Exactly. David is fooling around with the cop (Mathew St. Patrick), but he is terrified someone will find out. He is a real person who wrestles with issues that a lot of gay people still wrestle with these days.

Ball: Yeah. And here is somebody whose main obstacle in life is himself, and that's something that's very interesting to me. I get bored by television or entertainment that sort of presents gay characters as victims of such an oppressive society. I mean, yes, there are oppressive elements of society. But you make a choice to be a victim, and so I get really bored with those kinds of shows telling me, "Hey, America, it's OK to be gay!" Because duh. It's the same feeling I have when TV shows tell me it's bad to be a racist. It's like thanks for thinking I'm an idiot, and I can't figure that out on my own. But what really interests me is that internal struggle that someone like David has to go through because you don't see that on television.

Also, one of the things about David is he's religious. And as we go through the course of the season we touch on all the stuff that is going on in religions right now. To me, it's fascinating that these bureaucratic organizations have these meetings, and they're like, "Well, it's still not OK to be gay. We hate the sin. We love the sinner." I want to go, "You know what? You people don't have any authority here to separate me from God, and you can act like you can all you want, but it's such a fucking joke."

You don't really see that stuff on TV, or if you do, you see both sides presented in an issue of the week way. I wanted to get into it with a character having to wrestle with those demons himself because I had to wrestle with those demons myself at an earlier point in my life, and I was just as tormented and conflicted as he was. Getting to that point where I did come out was the healthiest, best thing I ever did.

Champagne: Can you give Gaywatch readers more of a preview of what will be happening in David's life over the course of the season?
Ball: David—because he is so conflicted and becomes more and more compartmentalized—actually becomes a deacon at his church, and at the same time he engages in a variety of compulsive behaviors. It's a wild ride, but it's very true because people like that who deny themselves and their true natures, they're the ones who get out of control. So, he's got a lot of lessons to learn.

Champagne: Tell me about the process of casting *Six Feet Under*. Was it difficult?
Ball: There were certainly moments were somebody came in, and I went, "OK, that's it." Richard Jenkins came in, and I was like, "That's Nathaniel. I don't need to see anybody else. That's it." But it was difficult to find the right people because the characters are more complex and less safe than a lot of characters you see on TV. So you need a specific kind of actor who can show you those things in a character psyche, and at the same time remain interesting, and I hate this word, but it's the only word I can use right now—likable. There were certain people who came in, and in their hands, for example, David became very unlikable. Or in their hands Brenda [who is played by Rachel Griffiths of *Hilary and Jackie* fame] was just a fucking, nightmare bitch from hell. But one of the great things about HBO is I was never pressured to cast somebody because they were pretty. I was never pressured to cast anybody because they had recognizable TV quality.

I have a tendency to believe that you start with the character, and then you find the best actor to fit the role. That's not always the way people think in Hollywood. It's like, "Oh my God. You can get such and such who had that sitcom seven years ago." And the writer's response may be, "But they're totally wrong for the role." And the studio and the network response is always, "We'll just change the role to fit them." Well, see, I'm a playwright, and that to me is like saying drive backwards in traffic without looking where you're going. It doesn't make any sense.

We live in such a cult of personality. I go to meetings, and I am constantly pitched actors as characters. They'll go, "Oh, we have this great idea. Winona Ryder is Goldie Hawn and Danny DeVito's daughter." I mean, I actually went to a meeting where somebody said that.

Champagne: You seem sane. How does a sane person survive in this crazy business?

Ball: It's not hard for me at all right now because I won an Oscar, and everybody pays attention to what I say. [He laughs.]

Champagne: But it must have been awful a few years ago before you won the Oscar.

Ball: It was really frustrating. It was infuriating. My year on *Grace Under Fire*. My three years on *Cybill*. Although I wouldn't trade them because I learned invaluable lessons, they were torture. It was like being a member of the court of some mad monarch who was completely insane and power mad and crazy and doing completely destructive things to the country, but nobody could say anything, and you had to traverse a minefield of politics.

Champagne: What is it like when you run into people nowadays? I'm talking about the people who treated you poorly. Do they kiss your ass now?

Ball: I did run into somebody who was an executive for a production company that I worked for. I ran into her at a restaurant in New York, and she was like, "Our little Alan," which was really offensive, but I didn't say anything. Then, she said something like, "You know, we'd still love for you to come in and pitch some ideas to us." I wanted to go, "Are you serious? I hated when I was at your company. I hate the way you do business, and I hate everything about your stupid company, and by the way I don't have to suck up to you now!" But I didn't. [He laughs.]

Big Mind, Small Screen: *Six Feet Under*'s Alan Ball

JEFF GREENWALD / 2004

From *Tricycle: The Buddhist Review*, Tricycle.com, Summer 2004. © 2004 Jeff Greenwald.
Reprinted by permission of the author.

"Of all footprints, that of the elephant is supreme," declared the Buddha in the *Great Nirvana Sutra*. "And of all mindfulness meditation, that on death is supreme."

Likewise: Of all situation comedies, *I Love Lucy* was the greatest; but of all prime-time series about impermanence, *Six Feet Under* is without peer. Nothing that has appeared on the small screen can compare with this quirky meditation on attachment, mortality, and—as series creator and executive producer Alan Ball puts it—"life, in the constant presence of death."

Though it makes no claims, *Six Feet Under* is a great example of how dharma themes are infiltrating American popular culture—without any direct Buddhist connection. Most of the show's twelve million-plus viewers will never attend a teaching or retreat, or travel to lands where the process of dying is viewed as an opportunity for liberation. Alan Ball's series doesn't pretend to instruct its audience about death. It simply lifts the veil from a subject too often viewed, in our culture, through filters of fear and ignorance.

Six Feet Under premiered on HBO in 2001, two years after Ball (who'd written previously for network sitcoms) won a Best Screenplay Oscar for his astonishing *American Beauty*. Like *American Beauty*, *Six Feet Under* deals with themes of transformation and redemption—with a darkly comic twist.

The series takes us into the lives of the Fishers, proprietors of a family-run funeral home in Los Angeles. In the pilot, Nathaniel Fisher, the family's patriarch, dies instantly when his new hearse is broadsided by a city bus. The Christmas Eve tragedy leaves Fisher's four survivors—his wife, Ruth; teenage daughter, Claire; and two adult sons, Nate (a free spirit, visiting from Seattle) and David (an anxious, closeted gay)—polarized and self-protective.

The show's foundation is the interplay of the Fishers, as each family member struggles toward the core of his or her identity amid an ever-changing caravan of corpses. Friends and lovers fill out their circle, each seeming to embody a classic obstacle (or ally) in the path to liberation. David Fisher's companion, Keith, is a black L.A. cop with anger issues; Nate's lover, Brenda, is a hungry ghost, plagued by an insatiable appetite for sex and sensation. Young Claire wrestles with the blithe ignorance of her high school peers. At the center of this mandala, the three-story Fisher & Sons Funeral Home is an unflinching reminder of the destination awaiting us all.

Every episode of *Six Feet Under* opens with a death, and with each death the Fishers, managing the burial, are given a lesson in transformation. The funeral of a Mexican gang member becomes a teaching on compassion and reconciliation; the passing of an elderly black woman leads into an exploration of True Nature. Some deaths are peaceful, some sudden, some the result of long illness. But all remind us of the fact that, as Larry Rosenberg writes in *Living in the Light of Death*, "No one is guaranteed even one more breath."

After three years of devoted fandom and intense discussions with my *Six Feet* sangha, I felt compelled to meet the force behind this extraordinary series. Alan Ball is a tall, contemplative man whose serious eyes are balanced by a large, infectious laugh. His understated office in the Sunset Gower studios is decorated with memorabilia from *American Beauty* and portraits of the *Six Feet Under* cast. The bookshelf is stacked with texts about death and dying, including several volumes by Thomas Lynch: a poet, philosopher, and funeral director.

When *American Beauty* was released, much was made of the film's Zen underpinnings—especially the scene where a simple plastic bag, dancing in a vortex of wind, is seen as a paradigm of perfection. Yet Ball, surprisingly, has no real Buddhist practice of his own.

"I've never been formally introduced to Buddhism," he reflects. "It's almost as if I have an instinctive predisposition toward it. I'm not very disciplined. I have a hard time meditating, but I keep trying to chip away at my resistance. But I do lean toward that discipline more than any other because, from what little I know of it, it seems to make the most sense."

Ball, forty-six, was raised a Methodist in Georgia. His introduction to Buddhist sensibilities arose—like Siddhartha Gautama's—from direct confrontation with mortality. "When I was thirteen years old," he says, "my sister died in a car accident. It was her twenty-second birthday. She was driving me to a music lesson; I was in the car with her. That brought me face to face with tremendous loss, and the impermanence of things. I struggled for years and years with how to cope with that—and, ultimately, I started developing an innate sense of detachment."

I ask Ball if he feels that the mere act of watching *Six Feet Under* can be a liberating experience, a way of coming to terms with our national denial of death.

"I would hope so," he replies. "Working on the show has certainly been a liberating experience for me."

"Has it helped you resolve any of your own issues regarding mortality? For your sister or for yourself?"

"It has. I was so wounded by my sister's death that I was afraid of intimacy, of getting close to another human being, because they might die on me. So I poured myself into my work. And I was alone for many, many years. Even though I can't possibly say that I've erased all my fear and anxiety about death, I've certainly erased any denial that it does indeed exist—and that it will happen to me."

Ball speaks with joy and optimism about his current relationship, which represents a huge step away from his terror of loss and dissolution. His ability to love is based not on repression of the truth, he says, but on an appreciation that all committed relationships exist within the confines of mortality—and the utter certainty that they must eventually end.

The central characters on *Six Feet Under* mirror Ball's growth. At the end of the first season, Nate Fisher (who suffers from severe headaches and nausea) is diagnosed with arterio-venous malformation (AVM), a mysterious disorder affecting blood vessels near the brain. Though AVM commonly goes undetected—causing little or no harm—the vessels can potentially rupture at any time, leading to a stroke or sudden death. Despite this Damoclean sword, Nate strives for deeper intimacy with his lover. The series thus becomes, for characters and viewers alike, a form of *maranasati*—the death-awareness contemplation studied in Theravada monasteries.

"Had I not been doing work of this nature," Ball admits, "it would have been harder for me to face my own mortality. If the sitcom I created for ABC (*Oh, Grow Up*) had become a hit and been syndicated for a gazillion dollars, and the main point of my life had become about being funny, I would have been less inclined to get into the muck of a meaningful life in this culture.

"My work is, for me, a spiritual discipline. I've been very blessed in that I've been given situations in which I can actually write about living life meaningfully."

Ball's evolution has made him one of the most celebrated screenwriters in America. I ask if his meteoric success within the Hollywood milieu has been an obstacle to his own spiritual progress.

"It's very seductive," he admits. "But whenever something happens to me, something else happens that puts things into perspective. The year I won the Oscar for *American Beauty*, I had also created *Oh, Grow Up*, which was universally loathed and reviled. One critic said it was actually 'painful' to watch. One issue of *People* magazine listed the Best and Worst of 1999. On one page were the Ten Best Movies, including *American Beauty*. If you turned the page, they listed the Ten Worst Television Shows—and *Oh, Grow Up* was one of them.

"I was very glad that happened. Because if you're going to do work that's meaningful—even if only to yourself—you have to maintain a certain level of humility and not take yourself too seriously. It's okay to take the work seriously—but not yourself."

In an Amazon.com interview, Ball observed, "We live in a culture that goes out of its way to deny mortality. And I think you have to have a deep and fundamental acceptance of mortality to really be able to see what's beautiful in life—because beauty and truth are inextricably connected."

Equating truth with mortality is an accurate view, but it's one that many Americans don't share. "Yet it is true," says Ball. "We die. And to live in a culture where people have surgery to avoid looking like they're aging, because we don't value wisdom as much as we value young skin—well, it seems hilarious." The absurdity is carried infinitely further, of course, when the compulsion to preserve appearances is carried into the grave. In one episode, a porn star's sudden demise reveals the extremes of such attachment, as Federico—the funeral home's virtuoso reconstruction artist—props up the woman's flopping silicone breasts with cans of cat food.

Such a typically American funeral, with a body "preserved" in a box, is radically different from Asian death ceremonies. Buddhist rites often climax with cremation, or, in the case of Tibetan Buddhism, "sky burial," a ritual in which the corpse is presented as an offering to birds and other animals. Ball, in the course of producing his show, "learned way more than I ever needed to know about what happens to bodies after we die." He now wishes to be cremated. I ask if he's ever seen a body burn. Indeed he has, during a trip to Bali.

"It's interesting," he laughs, "to look at my own karma. I run into funerals wherever I go. In the pilot episode of *Six Feet Under*, Nate recalls seeing a Sicilian funeral on a beach—that totally happened to me, when I was nineteen or twenty. Then there was Bali. And recently, when I went to Lebanon to visit my partner's family, we came across the burial of the people who had died in that plane crash from Africa to Lebanon. I see a pattern there. It's part of my work; it's part of my karma. It's part of what my consciousness is about."

One of the most interesting aspects of *Six Feet Under* is its refusal to take a stand on the afterlife. The Fishers (or the families of the deceased) may lock horns over their individual opinions on the subject, but the show itself does not. Sometimes, though, the dead visit individual members of the Fisher family, acting as foils for their inner dialogues. At the end of the pilot episode, Nathaniel Fisher appears at his own funeral for a word with his daughter. There's a delicious moment as, like the skeletal deity Chitipati, who dances upon charnel grounds, they chat up the benefits of being dead. Claire's priceless remark: "No more waiting to die."

"In the writers' room, we envision that, when the dead speak, they're not ghosts," says Ball. "They are the dead person's presence and memory and influence, in the mind of the person being spoken to."

Ball personally believes in reincarnation, but insists that the show remain neutral. "That's a personal choice that everyone makes," he asserts. "It's a mystery. It would be incorrect to have *Six Feet Under* say anything one way or the other."

Confronting death and dissolution is never easy, even for monks. Most lay practitioners will never engage in extreme Buddhist practices like *chöd*, in which one meditates with corpses, camps in charnel grounds, or stirs up vivid images of one's body in the process of decay. We will simply live our lives as best we can, balancing work and family with our NetFlix wish list and the occasional ten-day retreat.

The characters in *Six Feet Under* aren't monks, either; they're not even Buddhists. (Even Brenda, who surrounds herself with images of the Buddha and other protective deities, seems helpless in the face of her compulsions.) Still, their individual encounters with *samvega*—an urgent desire for liberation, inspired by a visceral encounter with samsara—are enormously moving and instructive. They illustrate Ball's conviction that "for a lot of people, a life that's filled with mistakes and tragedy and random messiness can be way more spiritual than a life of simple piety."

At the very least, *Six Feet Under* demonstrates how Buddhist sensibilities are steadily entering our consciousness; so much so that, as Ball implied, they are becoming "instinctual." It's as if Ball himself is simply a vehicle for this process, the embodiment of a Zen koan about nondoing.

"I don't feel like *I've* created these characters," he states with conviction. "The show and its characters have a life of their own that is very real. Part of my job is to get out of their way and let them show me what they need to do."

Alan Ball: *Six Feet Under*

ANNA CARUGATI / 2004

From WorldScreen.com, October 2004. Reprinted by permission of World Screen, Inc.

Alan Ball started his career writing plays in New York and then went on to Hollywood to work on network sitcoms. He hit it big writing the screenplay for the feature film *American Beauty*, which won the Academy Award for best movie and best original screenplay. The success of that movie caught the attention of HBO, which was looking for a series about how people deal with death. The result has been *Six Feet Under*, about a family-run funeral home, and people coping with loss and with each other.

Carugati: What creative freedom have you found at HBO?
Ball: There are three levels of artistic freedom. One is the relaxed broadcast standards. You can have nudity and profanity and you can have characters' sex lives being a major part of the story. That allows you to write a story line about someone combating sexual compulsiveness. The other level is that when HBO pitched this idea to me, Carolyn Strauss [the president of HBO Entertainment] said, "I want to do a show about America's relationship with death." No network is ever going to do that, because the network's main reason is to sell products. They want to create this world that puts you in this frame of mind to believe in stuff and be happy so you will go buy the products. When you remove the element of having to sell products, the show becomes something in and of itself, rather than becoming a means of delivering the advertisers' messages. That's a tremendous amount of freedom. The third level of freedom is that they respect the people they hire. They don't second-guess you; they don't give notes [suggesting changes in the script]. They don't spend a lot of time trying to take what you are creating and turn it into something else that looks like something that has been successful before. They want to broaden the scope of what television can be.

Carugati: What was your reaction when Carolyn Strauss said she wanted a series about a funeral home?

Ball: I was also doing a sitcom for ABC that was not very good. Everyone wanted to meet me after *American Beauty* opened, but I was busy. I didn't meet anybody. But when Carolyn Strauss from HBO called, I said, "Yeah, I'll meet with HBO," because *The Sopranos* had premiered and I was so jazzed by the show because I was seeing what television can be capable of. So I met with her, and she said, "I love your movie. I'm thinking about doing a show set in a family-run funeral home about America's relationship with death." And I thought, "What a fantastic idea." I had spent some time in funeral homes growing up, with the funerals of my family members. But I was doing the ABC show, and I said, "Best of luck with that, I wish I could do it but I am busy." And then my show got cancelled. I was very burned out. I was very upset that the show had been cancelled. I went home for the Christmas vacation, and I wrote a pilot. For me it was a catharsis, and it was a way of dealing with the show being cancelled. It's no accident that the pilot takes place over Christmas. I was visiting my mom. My house is haunted with the ghosts of my sister and my dad. And Christmas is always a time that makes that particularly difficult. I put it all into the script. I came back to Los Angeles. I called my agent. We took the pilot to HBO. They read it. They asked for a meeting. Carolyn said, "I loved this, I loved the characters, I feel it's a little safe. I'd like to see the whole thing be a little more fucked up." And I felt, "When are you ever going to get a note like that?!" [Laughs] And I thought, "I can do that." And I did a second draft.

Carugati: You experienced the loss of family members. How do you draw on personal experience and how do you move beyond the grief, letting life take its course?

Ball: There are two great quotes by C. S. Lewis in his book *A Grief Observed*. The first is, "No one ever told me grief felt so much like fear," and the second, which I may be misquoting, is, "The only way out of grief is through it." And in terms of my own personal experience, I lost my sister when I was quite young. I lost my father. A lot of that found its way into the pilot. Nate loses his father [who dies in a car accident]. My sister was killed in a car accident. [It was] very abrupt, very sudden and unexpected; it changed everybody's lives. That was my own experience and was put into the pilot.

Over the last four seasons, I've been able to work out a lot of my own fears about death and the finality of death, and the fact that it exists and it will happen to all of us. I can't say I'm not afraid of it, or I'm totally comfortable with it, but I'm very aware that it exists. I don't take that for granted. And working on the show has allowed me to reference a lot of that and has allowed me to open myself up to living more fully, surprisingly enough. And I do think that is the purpose of grief. When you've lost someone close to you, you lose a part of yourself, and you have to grieve for that and you have to let go of it. It feels like jumping off into the void; it feels terrifying, and it feels like you can't go on. But it is precisely those feelings that allow you to move through to the other side. And if you subvert them and you don't allow yourself to have those feelings, then you'll get stuck.

That's sort of what our show is about—people moving through not just dealing with death, but moving through all those passages in their lives, moving from one chapter to another, whether it's relationships, or family members or education or jobs or whatever. Life is a series of letting go and saying goodbye, which allows you to move forward and embrace something new.

Carugati: As a writer, is it more dramatic to be faced with fate or faced with choices?

Ball: It's much more dramatic to be faced with choices and challenges. If everything is predetermined, and you are just going through the motions, there's not much drama there. You are just reacting to what life gives you, to what is predetermined. Whereas if you are faced with confrontation and choices, and you know there are going to be consequences, you want to do the right thing. Many times doing the right thing is going to make life more difficult for you than actually doing the easier thing or the more ethically questionable thing. Being moral creatures, we are always faced with what is the right choice. I think that is much more dramatic.

Carugati: How do you keep the momentum of a series going, season after season?

Ball: It helps having seven other writers. They are very smart, very gifted, very talented, complex, unusual people, all of whom have their own histories, their own tragedies, their own affinities with different characters. So that helps a lot.

Carugati: How does that work? Do you give them the general outline of how you see each episode and then they flesh it out?

Ball: We get together as a group. It's oddly very democratic, with me having absolute veto power! [Laughs] We get together and we decide where we want each character to go over the course of the season. And then we broadly map out the twelve episodes of the season–it used to be thirteen, now it's twelve. And then we go through episode by episode and we map them out as a group, with me having the veto power and saying, "No I just don't buy that." Then one writer will go off and write one script, come back, and we give notes as a group. The writer then goes off and does a second draft. It comes back to me, and I'll do whatever pass I need to do on it. It used to be way more extensive the first couple of seasons, but all the writers have been with us now since season three. So everybody gets it, and knows the show and knows its voice. I don't have to do that much work.

Carugati: And no notes from HBO? How different is it from working for a broadcast network?

Ball: Oh, we get notes, but the difference is that the notes are smart and make the show better. Whereas during my experience at ABC, everybody felt like they had to give notes, just to justify their job. Basically, all the notes from ABC could be crystallized under two ideas: make everybody nicer and articulate the subtext. Have everybody explain what's going on with themselves emotionally. Removing subtext and making everybody nicer, removing conflict—where's the drama? It's flat. Watch most American TV and that's the way it is.

Carugati: Would you work for the networks again?

Ball: No. The only way I would work for the networks would be to have the same freedom I have now, and I don't think that's possible in commercial network TV in America [which is] so advertising-driven, because those shows have to prove themselves within the first three or four episodes.

Carugati: As a creator, how do you feel about that?

Ball: I think it's terrible.

Carugati: Doesn't a show need more time to find its voice?

Ball: Absolutely. You look at famous American shows. You look at *Cheers*— that could not happen today. *Seinfeld* could not happen today. Shows take time to find themselves, and that's in the best of all possible worlds. But when you have a hundred people giving notes—I had a point during ABC where people's assistants were coming up and giving me notes, like, "Don't you think it would be better if she blah, blah, blah," or "I don't like the color of the wall on that set." And I would think, "What do you want me to do? How much time do you want me to waste?" And the horrible thing about sitcoms is that you write a funny script, [the actors read through it and the network people] laugh at jokes the first time they hear them. The second day they laugh a little less, and by the third day they say, "That joke doesn't work anymore." And you say, "That's because you've heard it and you know what's coming. The audience hasn't." And then you have to rewrite the jokes. I'm very happy to be out of network television.

Carugati: Are you leaving *Six Feet Under* after this season, or are you staying?

Ball: I'm going to see how this season goes. I've always felt that if the show starts to feel stale, or it starts to run out of steam, I want to get out of there. I don't want it to drag on for years and years, and just be an empty shell of its former self.

Considering Alan Ball: An Interview

THOMAS FAHY / 2005

From *Considering Alan Ball: Essays on Sexuality, Death and America in the Television and Film Writings* (McFarland Press, 2006). Reprinted by permission of Thomas Fahy.

After attending Florida State University, Alan Ball moved to New York to pursue a career in the theater. With the help of several friends, he started Alarm Dog Repertory—a small theater company that produced many of his early plays, including *Bachelor Holiday*. But it wasn't until the successful production of *Five Women Wearing the Same Dress* that Ball's work caught the attention of Hollywood. In 1994, he was offered a job as a writer and executive producer for *Grace Under Fire* (1994–1995) and, one year later, for *Cybill* (1995–1998). Disillusioned by his experiences on these shows, Ball turned his attention to writing for the big screen. He began the screenplay for *American Beauty*, which would win the Academy Award for Best Original Screenplay in 1999 and would give him the opportunity to create the award-winning show *Six Feet Under* (2001–2005).

On July 29, 2005, I had the opportunity to talk with Alan Ball about his work and some of the issues raised in this collection, *Considering Alan Ball: Essays on Sexuality, Death and America in the Television and Film Writings*.

Fahy: I want to begin by asking a few questions about your early work in the theater. In 1984, you started a theater company in New York, Alarm Dog Repertory. How did that come about and what were some of artistic goals of Alarm Dog?

Ball: Well, I didn't start it myself. I started it with a lot of people I had known in college and in Florida where I lived prior to moving to New York. We basically were a group of actors, writers, and directors who loved to work. We had had similar companies in Florida, and also I had worked with a lot of these people in college. We just sort of found this vibe of working together, and it gave us something to do—rather than sitting around, going to auditions, and asking for permission to work. I've never been a big believer that you have to get other people to give you permission to work. I've always been a self-motivator, and even though I do have formal training, the majority of what I've learned has come from experience. From doing it yourself. So we didn't really have any formal goals, but we basically wanted to do new work that was either written by or developed by the company.

Fahy: How do you feel those experiences as a playwright and actor shaped your writing?

Ball: I think having some experience being on stage as an actor has made me very conscious of how I'm writing for actors. I think about what I myself might have a hard time saying, for example. It has also made me aware about what is stageable and what is possible. I did acting and writing and production stuff and publicity. All sorts of things. So I learned about what goes into making and producing a play. I also learned that it's important to get a sense for what the people who are working for you are doing and to respect it.

I love actors. I feel like my work really needs good actors because in the wrong hands it can be very . . . flat. It walks a line. And I really have a lot of respect for actors and the process.

Fahy: I'm also curious as to which playwrights and writers have influenced your work?

Ball: One person who has a lot of influence on me—just because I was exposed to his work at a very early age—is Tennessee Williams. Also being from the South myself and being gay myself, I think it spoke to me in many ways. I love the theatricality of it. I love the strong female characters. I feel there is an inherent sexism in most mainstream entertainment—in the movies more than anything else where women characters are basically just props or things to win or things to suffer and die horribly so that the hero will be motivated to seek vengeance. I also think the gay sensibility and the poetic outsiderness of Tennessee Williams's work was very influential.

I greatly admire the films of Robert Altman and Woody Allen as well.

Fahy: Woody Allen has such an amazing sense of place. He makes you feel like you're walking along the streets of New York in every scene.

Ball: Exactly. I also enjoy the playfulness of his films. When I first saw *Annie Hall* in college, I just loved the bittersweet sadness that ran through all of the comedy. I also admire his playfulness with form. All of those theatrical techniques that he uses—jumping into animation and having her get out of her body and watch him while she is having sex with him. All of those things influenced me, and I thought they were very creative.

Fahy: Looking back on some of your early plays, like *Made for a Woman, Five Women Wearing the Same Dress,* and *Bachelor Holiday,* what do you consider to be some of the most important themes and issues driving those works?

Ball: Well, I don't tend to think of my work that way. My process is much more mysterious to me, and I kind of like it that way because then it becomes a journey of discovery as opposed to having an outline and writing a term paper. But having been interviewed a lot about my work now, I sort of feel like the overriding theme that interests me is the difficulty that people have trying to live an authentic life in this country.

Fahy: Your characters in *American Beauty* and *Six Feet Under* certainly struggle with this.

Ball: Yes. And with the saturation of the media and the unbelievable levels of denial on all fronts that we live with in America—denial of the truth, denial of death, denial of aging, and denial of what our culture really is (which is basically a corporatocracy and a welfare state for the rich)—I think it is increasingly difficult to live an authentic life. The levels of denial are so pervasive and so entrenched that I feel like the human spirit yearns to be authentic. But it's so hard. We don't want to see these problems. We don't want to talk about them.

Fahy: Do you think the medium of television is particularly effective for addressing these problems?

Ball: Well, I think the medium of television can be very powerful when it is used effectively, but I also think we get a very skewed perspective from it. The television media is often very self-serving for the ruling class. It's sad. People know they're being lied to. They either can't deal with it and they have this knee-jerk, Jesus patriotism, or they just become cynical. If you really sit down and look at what's happening in the world, it's so painful. We're destroying our planet. Our high standard of living is being paid for by people all across the globe. It is really painful to realize that. And we don't want to talk about it at all. It's a big house of cards, and if you really acknowledge the truth about what's going on, our entire system collapses. We're basically thugs and rapists and exploiters.

At the same time, who wants to drop out of life? There is a real tension that is created by living in the society that we live in and having human independence. We are so often defined by what we do and not by who we are in America.

Fahy: How have you addressed this tension in your writing?

Ball: A lot of my early work in the theater was a satire of corporations. And it was theatrical and funny and sketchy, but ultimately I don't think it was about actual characters, actually recognizable people. Also at that time, I was working in a corporation, so I had a tremendous amount of anger about that. Technically, I believe I'm still working for a corporation—one of the more insidious ones. But I'm pretty much left alone, and I get to do work that I find meaningful. So I don't have that same kind of frustration.

Fahy: I also want to ask about the role of art in your work. Both Ricky Fitts and Claire Fisher seem to be most comfortable in the world when they're taking pictures of it. Could you talk a little bit about artist figures in your writing? Why they are so important? How they contribute to some of the larger themes in your writing?

Ball: Again, that's not a conscious choice. I think I consider myself an artist, and I aspire for the work that I do to be art. I don't really know what that word means. My work for me is the closest thing I have to a religion. It is a discipline that is very meaningful, and it allows me to process what it means to be alive and what it means to be human. So I guess it is no mistake that I like characters who are exploring life through art.

I've veered away from characters who are writers because I find them to be really tedious. But I definitely have always had a creative bent. Even as a small child, I was doing and creating things.

Fahy: You have a lot of fun with psychiatry in your play *Your Mother's Butt*. Of course, we see a much broader portrait of psychiatry and the therapy industry in *Six Feet Under*. From self-help books to The Plan, therapy is . . . unpredictable at best. How would you characterize the role of therapy in *Six Feet Under*?

Ball: I have conflicted feelings about the therapeutic process. On the one hand, I've been in therapy on and off for at least half of my life, and it has been very beneficial. On the other hand, it encourages a kind of narcissistic navel-gazing, a self-involvement that is one of the biggest afflictions in our culture. A lot of us have lost the ability to just be instinctive, to live spontaneously. At the same time, had I not gone to therapy, I probably would have descended into some self-destructive behavior or become some sort of an addict. I was really in a lot of pain, and I didn't understand it. I needed help figuring it out.

Again, I don't make a conscious choice for characters to be in therapy or to be therapists. In my life, I have known people who are therapists. I have known a lot of people in therapy. I have been in therapy myself. I know people right now who are going to school to become therapists. So that stuff becomes part of my writing. I basically write about the world that I know. Things that find their way into the show come from some place in my life.

The controversial episode of *Six Feet Under* where David was kidnapped . . . that happened to my brother's girlfriend. The AVM condition that Nate Fisher had . . . my cousin had that. I know a lot of people who have died. A lot of people in my family have died. And that's just where it comes from. This is the world that I know. These are the things that the people I know have to deal with.

Certainly, if one of my themes is about the struggle to live authentically, therapy for a lot of people is a real step along the way, but at the same time, it can be its own trap. It's like everything. It works, and it doesn't work. There is good, and there is bad. It always comes down to balance.

Fahy: So what's next for you? Do you see yourself returning to television?
Ball: I actually do have an idea for a series that I wouldn't mind developing and creating. I don't want to run a show any time soon just because it is really grueling and exhausting. And I'm interested in pursuing things on the feature-side for a while.

I definitely think TV is a great medium because you get to spend a really long time with characters. You can see them grow and change over time in a way that is realistic. You don't have to cram everything into two hours. It is probably the closest I'll ever come to writing a novel. Even though saying that, I didn't write all of *Six Feet Under*. I had several writers that I worked with. I never could have done it myself. They had perspectives and experiences that I never could have brought to the table.

Also, I recently wrote my first play in ten years. That was a really great experience. It felt so relaxing to be able to lay back and luxuriate in language. Because I'm an avid reader—I read much more than I watch TV and go to the movies—it is so nice just to write a scene that lasts for twelve pages. To have a character start talking and talk for a really long time because what they're trying to express is complicated and they have all kinds of different feelings about it. So I really enjoyed that. I miss the theater. My playwriting career was just really starting to get off the ground when I got the offer to come out here and work in television.

I would love to be able to continue to work in all three mediums. I even have a dream of maybe one day actually writing a novel. I have a much easier time with dialogue than I do with prose, so I don't know if that is going to happen or not. It's a dream.

Fresh Air Interview with Alan Ball: A *Six Feet Under* Postmortem

TERRY GROSS / 2005

From *Fresh Air*, NPR, August 23, 2005. Interview reproduced with permission of WHYY, Inc.

Gross: This is *Fresh Air*. I'm Terry Gross. I'm one of the fans of HBO's *Six Feet Under* who really miss the characters now that the series has ended. We invited back the creator of the series, Alan Ball, to talk with us about bringing the series to a close. He wrote and directed the final episode. He also wrote the screenplay for *American Beauty*.

Before we go any further, a couple of disclaimers. If you're waiting to watch a tape of the final episode and don't want to know what happens, you might want to tape this interview and hold off listening until after you've watched the conclusion. And if you've never watched the show, well, I apologize if the interview is a little "insie."

Alan Ball has described *Six Feet Under* as a show about life in the face of death and about a family who, because of their work running a funeral home, is surrounded by death. At the conclusion of the final episode, the extended family begins to emerge from their grief over Nate's death. Here they are, sitting around the table toasting him.

(Soundbite of *Six Feet Under*)

Alan Ball, welcome back to *Fresh Air*. Well, how do you feel now that it's all over?

Ball: I feel a great sense of relief. I feel like I've been through a grieving process of my own. I feel like actually making the final four to five episodes of the show was kind of like a real excursion into grief, and the final episode was sort of coming out on the other side. And, you know, looking back, I sort of realize I guess that was my intent. My process is not quite so conscious, but I think now that's probably what the show itself was trying to do, to . . .

Gross: What, to put us all through the grieving process?

Ball: Or not so much to put people through it, but to go through it itself almost, you know what I mean? I mean, I'm kind of crazy. I do look at the show as a living entity that has its own will, that sometimes I—my job is to just really get out of the way of that and not try to form it into something.

Gross: Now I kept thinking—I mean, I would really spend a lot of time coming up with alternate endings. The ending where everybody's lives are totally screwed up, everybody's completely damaged. And then the happier version. And I was wondering how messy the ending was going to be and how much trouble there would be for the characters, and with the exception of Nate dying, things resolved pretty nicely. Why did you want to resolve things with—you know, with reasonably happy endings for everybody?

Ball: Well, because I feel like the final stage of grief—and if anything, I've sort of looked at the show as a meditation on grief. The final stage of grief is coming out of it and sort of reconnecting with life. I don't, for a minute, believe that these people moved forward and their lives were without drama and without conflict and without pain, without struggle. We just didn't see that.

But certainly, you look at what happens and, certainly, you know, I think David is devastated by the death of Keith. It wasn't as clear in the final montage, but Brenda had two husbands after Nate. I mean, I don't think those relationships were easy. I don't necessarily think Ruth and George lived happily ever after. And Claire came back to her mother's funeral when she was in her mid-forties and reconnected with Ted. Who knows what happened in those years up till then? Were there other marriages?

Gross: Oh, is that how they get reconnected? Okay.

Ball: Yeah.

Gross: It all goes by so quickly in that closing collage I could hardly keep up.

Ball: But I feel like at the moment when Claire leaves to go off to the—you know, into her new life, that's where those people are at that time, but [. . .] I never felt like, OK, everything's tied up in a nice little package.

Gross: Right.

Ball: I just felt like, well, they've come out of the—they've started to come out of the tunnel of Nate's death, and she's leaving and something new is starting, and that's the end of this show.

Gross: The website actually has obituaries for the main characters which kind of details some of the things that happened to them later in life, in their lives past the end of the series. Can you talk a little bit about the process of sitting down alone or with other members of the writing staff to figure out what the final fate of the characters was going to be and to even write lives past the end of the series for them?

Ball: Well, we reconvened back in August, I guess about a year ago, to start figuring out what the final season was going to be, and within the first week, somebody had pitched—I wish I could remember, because I felt like it was such a great idea, that we actually see the deaths of all the characters. And so it just felt so organically appropriate to the show, and there was a lot of conflict in the room about whether Nate should or shouldn't die. And I was open to him not dying, but I'm very instinctive, and I just went, "Pitch me something that is as effective or as—you know, works as organically and fits within—and is what would be the final chapter of this if it were a big long novel. Pitch it to me." And nobody was able to. So once—I didn't—we didn't want to kill Nate in the very last episode. We wanted to see the family deal with the grief and the loss and see how Nate's life, now that it was actually finished, at least in this plain, how it would affect those who loved him and those whom he loved.

Gross: Before Nate dies, he and his wife Brenda are fighting all the time, and then Nate starts to fall in love with Maggie, who's the daughter of his mother's estranged husband. And he dies of this brain condition that he has just after he and Maggie have sex for the first and only time. Why did you and the writers want him to die at such a morally messy moment?

Ball: Well, personally—I can't speak for the other writers—but I think one of the things that appealed to us throughout the production of the show is things that were morally messy, because to me, that seems to be so much more of what life is about than this facsimile of life that we see depicted on television, which is always about these very clear-cut moral choices and these very clearly defined heroes and villains and this world in which people really do sort of figure things out and live these really manageable lives. Now I don't know if I'm so far out of the mainstream that that just doesn't make sense to me or if it doesn't actually make sense to most people.

Gross: In your mind, if Nate had lived, would he and Maggie have become lovers? Would that have been the true love in his life or do you think that would have ended, too, and . . .

Ball: In my mind, I'm not sure that had he lived, he and Brenda really would have split up. I think he was feeling something very deeply and passionately at that moment, and he expressed it and then he died, and there's something really deeply tragic in that, which I'm drawn towards in terms of drama, in terms of telling a story. I mean, I think had he left Brenda and gone with Maggie, I think she would have had a real hard time living up to what he saw in her. I think possibly had he stayed with Brenda, it might have been the thing that really brought them together and they were able to move forward and actually into a new and different place. It may have just been a placeholder, and then later, something else would have happened on both their parts. I mean, Brenda was in sort of a better place at the time when the series ended, but she certainly had her own streak of confusion that could have led her to different places.

Gross: Now Brenda and her brother, Billy, are very close, but he actually seems to be truly in love with her during part of the series. And she has to physically rebuff him at some point. But in I think it's next to the last episode, there's a sequence where they actually start to physically touch in a sexual way. And I was so relieved when Brenda wakes up and it's just a dream.

Ball: (Laughs)

Gross: And everyone I spoke to about that scene said exactly the same thing: "I'm so glad it was just a dream." Can you talk a little bit about what went on in the writers' room about that scene and whether to do it and so on?

Ball: Well, there were actually people in the writers' room saying, "Brenda and Billy just really—we just need to get them together and just let them be together." And, of course, there were people in the writers' room who were pitching at the season four that there actually was a nuclear holocaust and that . . .

Gross: (Laughs)

Ball: . . . season five took place in a nuclear wasteland. So I said, "No, I don't think that's going to be a satisfying experience for our audience, and I also don't think it's right for the show." These two saved each other's lives growing up with these kind of mythically horrible, Greek tragedy monsters of parents that they have. And so Craig Wright, a very talented writer, was the writer who that episode was assigned to. And we knew we wanted it to go on so long that you actually got really physically uncomfortable and you thought, "Oh, my God, this is really happening" before she woke up from the dream.

And Craig went off to write his first episode, and he brought it back. And I remember I read the episode and the line where Billy goes, "This is what your penis would look like if you were a boy." And I had this moment of revulsion, and I thought, "I'm not sure we can go there." But every other writer at that table said, "We have to go there." That's what's so exciting about this moment—is because you really do see the truth of what is there on some subconscious level about their—you know, part of that weird attraction between them that was formed when they were children, with these wildly sexually inappropriate parents and friends acting out all around them, is that they felt like they were each other. And I said, "OK. You know, I'll trust you. I'll trust you guys on this."

Gross: Have you gone to many funerals since *Six Feet Under* started?

Ball: I haven't. I actually—I mean, certainly people I know have died. I—but because of my schedule, I haven't been able to attend. And, also, I avoid funerals. Funerals are very painful experiences for me because the first funeral I ever went to was—it was for my great-aunt, and my mother started weeping. And I realized I had never seen my mother cry—says a lot about my family, which also sort of explains where the Fishers come from.

And then shortly after that it was my sister's funeral, which just was a deeply, deeply horrible, traumatic, surreal experience for me. And not long after that, my grandfather died. And there were six grandsons, and somebody thought it would be a really great idea for the grandsons to serve as pallbearers. And I just—I have a thing with funerals. I don't—it's a deeply, deeply painful experience for me to go. And I'm sort of ashamed to admit that I haven't been to a funeral since *Six Feet Under* started.

Gross: Do you explain all this to people who expect you to come?

Ball: I don't. I don't think I've explained it to them that way. I just say, you know, "I can't make it because I'm working," but, you know, I'll send flowers or donations or whatever, and I certainly communicate with the survivors. But I've never been able to actually make it to the actual service. And, you know, each character on *Six Feet Under* has a little thing about them that is just really not likeable and not admirable, and I guess this is one of mine.

Gross: You know, you mentioned that the first time you saw your mother cry was at your grandparent's funeral. And is your mother—and you said that's where the Fisher family comes from—was your mother much like Ruth in any way?

Ball: In some ways. Ultimately Ruth became her own character and her own creation. My mom is very different from her. She's got a much more wicked sense of humor. She's earthier. She never was repressed in quite the same way. But certainly there are bits and pieces of my family and myself in all of these characters, as is true for all the other writers as well.

Gross: I want to clear up a plot point that confuses me and I know confuses some other people. Do you, as the creator of this series, know for sure who Maya's father is? Was it Nate, or was it Lisa's brother-in-law?

Ball: Do I know for sure who her biological father is? No, no, I don't. And I also don't really know what happened between Hoyt and Lisa when she died. I don't really know exactly what went on there, and that—part of what we wanted to dramatize is: What about those things that you never really know?—because I think, you know, part of what consciousness and society and certainly our modern consumer-, media-driven society has done is it's given us the idea that there are answers to everything and that you can know everything. And what gets ironed out by that kind of concept is mystery, you know. And I think, at the risk of sounding really stupid, there is so much that we will never be able to comprehend; that we don't even have the senses to comprehend.

And I think part of living a spiritual life is being OK with not knowing answers that you can't get. Was Maya Nate's biological daughter? We don't really know. Was she his daughter? Yes. He was her father. Ultimately whether or not his DNA is in that child is not as important as did he love her to the best of his ability and see her as his child and make her welfare something more important than his own?

Gross: Was it hard to keep the ending a secret?
Ball: Yes.

Gross: What did you do to make sure it stayed a secret?
Ball: Well, you know, everybody in the series was told, "This is really important. It's really important that this is a secret and that we keep it a secret." All of our scripts were numbered, so that if somehow we could trace the script, that person would get in trouble. I don't know what kind of trouble they could actually get into. At some point we even went as far as to leak some purposely false spoilers onto the Internet. But even so, you know, some information found its way into the Internet if you knew where to look—people on some obscure site, which my assistant looked up. I tend to avoid those sites because they're just too confusing to me. They had it nailed that Nate dies in episode nine and that in the final episode you see everybody's death. And I sort of went, "Well, you know, I hope not everybody goes to that website," and, fortunately, I don't think that many people do.

Gross: Very devious of you to have misled the public with false information on the Internet.
Ball: Well, that's because there was some stuff getting out during season three, and we actually went so far in season three as to—and we figured out that where it was coming from was when pages of the script were faxed to casting directors' offices or agents' offices that people were getting bits and pieces and posting that on the Internet. So we actually went so far as to fax false pages. We would fax the actual scenes that were being auditioned, but then in the next scene it would say—you would see—or in the scene prior to it, on the first half of the page before the actual scene started, we would say things like, you know, "Ruth collapses and is rushed to the hospital," or Ruth would turn to somebody and go, "How can I be pregnant at this age?" or something like that.
Gross: (Laughs)
Ball: Just because you don't want it to get out there 'cause you don't want it—I mean, certainly a big appeal, I think, of the show was that it didn't take you

where you expected it to take you, hopefully, in the way that life does that. So, I mean, I felt like we had to be devious.

Gross: So what's next for you? What are you working on now?

Ball: Well, interestingly, I just got back from Dartmouth College in New Hampshire, where I was doing a workshop of a new play that I've written with the New York Theatre Workshop, first play I've written in ten years. And we worked on it for about a week with some great actors, a terrific director, Jo Bonney, and did a reading of it in front of an audience, and it went very, very well, so I'm definitely going to pursue that.

I'm also in the process of adapting a novel, a novel called *Towelhead*, by Alicia Erian, a novel that was published last year. It's a great, great story, and I want to finish the screenplay by the end of September in the hopes of directing it sometime next year. And I'm in the process of finishing up a deal with HBO to develop some new TV.

Gross: Oh, good. Good. Well, Alan Ball, thank you for *Six Feet Under*. I'm sorry it's over. I'm really glad you did it.

Ball: Well, thank you. Thank you very much. And I love talking to you.

Sexual Politics and Awakenings in *Towelhead*

CYNTHIA LUCIA / 2008

From *Cineaste Magazine*, July 2008. Reprinted by permission.

Sexual abuse in adolescence, the received wisdom has it, will permanently scar, or destroy, the victim. While the psychologically damaging effects are undeniable, not every instance of abuse results in the permanent debilitation that our "victim culture"—as fueled by TV talk shows and their investment in "dramatic" revelation—would condition us to believe. The complexities and gray areas surrounding sexuality and human desire present multiple variations and outcomes, a subject Alicia Erian explores in her 2005 novel *Towelhead*, recently adapted for screen and directed by Alan Ball. Although *Towelhead* represents his directorial debut, Ball has an already-established and impressive track record as a playwright, as the award-winning screenwriter of *American Beauty* (1999), and as creator/producer (and sometime writer/director) of the highly acclaimed television series *Six Feet Under*, that ran on HBO from 2001 to 2005.

Ball's adaptation of *Towelhead* captures both the drama and humor of Erian's very engaging novel as it explores the sexual awakening of Jasira, a thirteen-year-old girl whose beauty and developing body imply a maturity beyond her years. Her sexuality, and the charge it delivers, confuses Jasira and causes family tension—sparking the insecurities of her mother Gail (Maria Bello) and the authoritarian anger of her father Rifat (Peter Macdissi), whose Lebanese background demands modesty and restraint.

From the beginning, the film poses questions that continue to resonate and for which there are no clear or easy answers. *Towelhead* opens with Jasira standing in the bathtub in her bathing suit, shaving cream slathered on her inner thighs, as her mother's live-in boyfriend Barry (Chris Messina)—razor in hand—assures her that she'll no longer have kids teasing her in gym class. This will be their little secret, he says, since Gail does not allow Jasira to shave. Is Barry stepping over a line when he helps Jasira in her articulated desire or is he simply being fatherly, empowering her to protect herself at school? When Gail finds pubic hair clogging the bathroom drain and learns the whole story, she forces Jasira from their Syracuse home to live with Rifat—a NASA engineer— in Houston, saying that by living with a man, maybe Jasira will learn how to behave properly around them. Concerned with her own happiness first, Gail offers little comfort in telling Jasira that she loves her, while simultaneously declaring that "this whole thing is your fault," as Jasira cries in her arms at the airport.

The very fault lines of conscious knowledge, unconscious power, and unintended consequences shape the volatile landscape that the novel and the film create. In the novel, Jasira is aware that Barry's help is more than fatherly, with the first line reading, "My mother's boyfriend got a crush on me, so she sent me to live with Daddy." In the film, upon moving to Houston, Jasira gradually becomes aware of a certain power her sexuality confers, but as true of any girl her age, she has little sense of what will happen or what it will mean as men react to it.

Played by the eighteen-year-old Summer Bishil in a wonderfully nuanced performance, Jasira is a burgeoning young woman and a little girl; she is awkwardly honest in expressing and acting upon desire yet frightened and guilt-stricken by it. She both embraces and resists her own sexual fantasies, kindled by her almost daily perusal of the *Playboy* magazines owned by Mr. Vuoso (Aaron Eckhart), a Houston neighbor and father of the boy she babysits. Shot in brilliant color and raucous speed, Jasira's fantasies of *Playboy* models riding topless in golf carts—laughing and frolicking while under the gaze of male photographers—are sweetly innocent but nonetheless sexual in their expression of imagined approbation, liberation, and pleasure. Unconsciously crossing and moving her legs while reading, Jasira experiences her first orgasm, a maneuver she will consciously repeat many times, both with and without the help of *Playboy*, as she sits in French class or at the lunch table in school.

The push-and-pull of surreptitious desire and nagging guilt is matched by Jasira's inconsistent and contradictory world. Her father is both caring and abusive—he violently and unexpectedly slaps her for wearing only an oversized T-shirt and underwear to the breakfast table, yet he seems not to notice that his girlfriend Thena (Lynn Collins) wears only his oversized dress shirt, as they nuzzle and kiss when Jasira first meets her. Jasira is surrounded by a media culture obsessed with female sexuality yet rife with sexual repression—made palpable by the stark sterility of the Houston suburb where she and her father live. This neatly mowed burial ground for creativity, hope, and aspiration is also a breeding ground for petty competition and prejudice. When Army reservist Vuoso installs a flagpole on his lawn, just as Bush the First invades Iraq, Rifat, a Lebanese Catholic, installs his own American flag, but illuminated by a floodlight, asserting his hatred for Saddam and stronger patriotism as an American citizen who is scrutinized through the lens of Vuoso's anti-Arab sentiment.

While there is genuine humor in moments like these, the 1990–91 setting situates Jasira's sexual awakening in the context of the Gulf War that, while never the center of the story, lingers hauntingly around its margins, implying that the larger imperialist hypocrisies of the political can't help but inform the personal. Although Mr. Vuoso's young son Zack (Chase Ellison) is likely verbalizing his father's unspoken prejudices (or those spoken behind closed doors) when he calls Jasira a "towelhead" and a "camel jockey," Mr. Vuoso's growing attraction to Jasira seems born of sincere affection, mingled with the heady surge of youthful masculine power it reawakens. He knows what he's doing when he knocks on her door after his wife and Zack leave for the day and seeing that Rifat isn't home, yet he genuinely feels the fear and error of his actions. Jasira is drawn to Mr. Vuoso and knows the power she exerts, yet is frightened by what transpires and feels guilty about her strong attraction to him, believing that somehow it is all her fault—as her mother had said of the much less serious incident with Barry.

The film exposes the painful emotions and contradictory messages that are at once personal, political, and cultural when Jasira confides to her neighbor Melina (Toni Collette)—a mother-to-be who befriends and supports her—that she acted like she wanted Mr. Vuoso to do the things he did because she thought she was supposed to act that way. In the novel she is constantly torn between feeling sorry for him and wanting to make him feel sorry for what he has done to her.

Neither the novel nor the film let Mr. Vuoso off the hook—there is no question that he behaved criminally, that he should have known better, and that he betrayed the trust Jasira placed in him as a friend and as an adult. But he is not represented as a monster. We see the distorting and deadening effects of a repressive, middle-class consumerist culture—certainly never presented as an excuse but as a condition that generates self-loathing and bigotry. When Mr. Vuoso spies Jasira's teenage boyfriend Thomas (Eugene Jones) leaving her house one afternoon, he is overcome by jealousy and driven by the need to possess her, a drive intensified by the fact that Thomas is African American— also fueling Rifat's racism when he forbids Jasira to continue seeing Thomas. Upon discovering that Jasira is not a virgin, Thomas proclaims without qualm or reservation, "That was my blood, not his," and suggests that maybe he and Jasira should no longer have sex, supporting Ball's contention that Jasira's character "becomes the embodiment of the racial, sexual, and political agendas of the different men in her life."

But, through all of it—and as a result of what she's experienced—Jasira is able to say, "I don't want to stop. I like having sex with you . . . I don't want to lose that because of what Mr. Vuoso did." Her honest self-assertion speaks volumes about Jasira's strength and character—and her growth—as do her words in the novel, upon encountering Mr. Vuoso, who has been indicted and released on bail. "I knew that I loved him," she admits. "I would never tell Melina or anyone else, but it was true. I couldn't help it. He was sorry. He really was. He hadn't meant to hurt me. He loved me, too." On the one hand these words could be seen as reflecting continued adolescent confusion; on the other hand, they could be read as reflecting a maturity of insight and genuine forgiveness—a reading the novel more strongly supports.

Unlike the visually explicit approach of French filmmaker Catherine Breillat in *Fat Girl* (2001), also a story of sexual awakening, Alan Ball approaches *Towelhead* with great restraint, conscious of not wanting to undermine the emotional journey of his character or its impact upon viewers. Faces dominate scenes of sexual intimacy, allowing Summer Bishil and Aaron Eckhart to explore and express the complex interplay of flirtation, desire, manipulation, fear, and recrimination that Jasira and Mr. Vuoso experience. Much of the rest of the film is photographed in long shot, positioning characters in the confines of their suburban homes and lawns as they attempt to find some small space within which to negotiate their uncertain emotional lives.

Cineaste spoke with Alan Ball in July about his vision in *Towelhead* and his work as a screenwriter and in television, during the shooting of *True Blood*, his new series for HBO slated to begin airing in September.

Cineaste: What drew you to Alicia Erian's novel?
Alan Ball: It just felt so real to me, and I loved that it presented this messy, morally complicated story without judging the characters. Also, it's the first time I've read a book about a young girl who undergoes an abusive relationship with an older man—or if not directly abusive, then certainly inappropriate because there's such a huge power imbalance—and she isn't destroyed for life. There was something so refreshing about that and something so true about the way she regarded him. As I read the book, I was thinking, "Oh, this isn't going to be good, it's not going to turn out good," and then when it actually did turn out good, I had such a genuine emotional reaction of relief and a kind of hopefulness. This is pretty rare for me, at least with books I read.

Cineaste: How did you work with Summer Bishil (who plays Jasira) and Aaron Eckhart (who plays Mr. Vuoso) in capturing the delicate complexities in their emotional and sexual relationship?
Ball: Basically, it was all there in Alicia's book; I did the best I could in transferring it to the screenplay. We did some rehearsing before we started shooting, but not too much, because I think those moments of discovery should happen while the cameras are rolling. Summer had just turned eighteen, and I thought, "This is going to be tough for her," but Summer is a very smart, very grounded young woman who has grown up all over the world—her vision of life is perhaps not as insulated as that of a teenager who has grown up

in America, watching American television and movies and never really getting outside of the country. I just worked with her on what it's like to be a very attractive young woman who's just coming into her sexuality and living in a world that denies her any pleasure or power. What is she going to do? She's going to seek pleasure and power. And there's nothing wrong with seeking pleasure and power, but in a perfect world, you would have adult role models who would help you make responsible decisions and give you the kind of perspective you need. But she's a kid.

Summer is an amazing actress who really understood this character. Frankly, I just had to point the camera in her direction and sort of nudge her more towards where I thought the story was when she was going a little off track. The great thing about her is that she actually said, "I was just happy to get a call-back," when people would ask, "What did you do when you thought about approaching this role?" We did use a body double a lot.

Cineaste: Can you talk about what guided your choices in the sex scenes between Jasira and Mr. Vuoso, which are both layered and edgy, to say the least, but visually restrained?

Ball: That was instinct. When I sent the script out, there was a disclaimer page at the beginning that said there would be no nudity, except for the *Playboy* fantasy scenes—because the really interesting story is about what's happening with these characters emotionally. The camera has to remain on their faces, because, especially when you're dealing with an underage character, you just can't go there—not because it's taboo but because it will take you out of what's happening for her emotionally, and I didn't want to do that. I felt like it would be too creepy for me to direct, much less for people to watch. Jasira's story is kind of heroic, I think. At the risk of sounding somewhat clichéd and "Hollywood," I think it's about a triumph of the human spirit, and I didn't want to detract from that in any way.

Cineaste: While you train your camera on faces during the intimate scenes, many other scenes are framed in long shot—often in deep focus. Can you discuss what you had in mind with the overall visual design of the film?

Ball: I believe in saving close-ups for when they're earned. I also feel you can communicate a lot by composition within the frame, much the same way great painters or photographers can tell a whole story by capturing one moment. I was very fortunate to be working with the great cinematographer Tom Sigel, who instinctively knows how to frame a shot to tell the story of what's happening emotionally for these characters.

Cineaste: Are you a filmmaker who does extensive storyboarding? Do you find yourself looking through the camera or even operating the camera?

Ball: I never operate the camera, I don't know how. I leave that to the people who are really good at it. Of course I look through the camera at times, but the monitor is my main way of seeing the movie as we shoot.

Cineaste: The novel is presented entirely from Jasira's point of view, but film, by its very nature, requires a certain juggling of visual perspectives. I noticed you use a wonderful motif of the window blind to alter point of view—there are moments when we see Jasira's visual point of view, as she steals glances through her window of Mr. Vuoso on his lawn, moments when Mr. Vuoso catches glimpses of Jasira in the same way, and when their neighbor Melina sees the two of them together. The motif also says something about the suburban milieu in which the characters live.

Ball: The suburban setting is from the novel. I like the notion of this brand-new, sterile, artificial landscape because I feel like that's one of the reasons why things like this happen so much—as a culture we're strangely terrified of sex and nature. I think the choices to use similar motifs with Jasira and Mr. Vuoso were intentional because in many ways, they're in the same boat.

However, he is an adult and must be judged by harsher standards because he knows better, but he is also somebody who has lost any sense of pleasure or power, and she awakens that in him. When I first met with Aaron, he said, "I don't want to play a pedophile." And I said, "Well, I don't really think this guy *is* a pedophile in that I don't think there is a fetishized sexualization of children going on in his psyche; I don't think he's ever looked at little girls in this way; I don't think he hangs around elementary schools. He's just a guy who is trapped in an emotionally arid life and doesn't know quite how he got there or how to get out, if it's even possible to get out. Probably as a young man he was totally IT and beautiful young girls were throwing themselves at him all the time. Now he's this cruising-toward-middle-age copy-store owner, and he's just lost all sense of connection to life, to anything. When he meets Jasira, she awakens this sense of being young and alive and powerful in him, and it's intoxicating.

Cineaste: Yes, his disappointment—in himself, his life—is palpable. During the Mexican restaurant scene you allow each character a privileged moment. As Mr. Vuoso goes into the men's room, we see him trying to come to terms with his own desire—his real fear and anticipated pleasure in it—and we see Jasira who is like a kid playacting an adult scene but also a young woman growing in her genuine insight about what one might call "sexual politics." The privileged moment you allow Mr. Vuoso is not present in the novel. What did you have in mind in allowing both characters these moments?

Ball: Quite honestly, the decision to give Mr. Vuoso his private moment in the bathroom was motivated by expediency. It was a way to keep from leaving Jasira at the table too long by herself and having the waiter bring their dinners, as that didn't seem that interesting, although I did have a draft where the waiter flirted with her in Spanish, but we had already played the beat of people assuming she was Mexican. I love that moment now with Aaron in the bathroom; it's one of my favorite moments in his performance and in the film.

Cineaste: I guess this brings us back to the issue of why Jasira's experience with Mr. Vuoso, while certainly upsetting, is ultimately something she is able to come to terms with and gather strength from. It seems to have something to do with his character in the sense that they are both struggling with their emotions in similar ways.

Ball: Yes, I think so. One of the things I love about the story and I loved about the book is that had Jasira not undergone this experience with Mr. Vuoso, she never would have been able to extricate herself from another abusive relationship with her father. It reflected the way traumatic experiences can sometimes lead to a greater understanding and freedom in life. One might even call that "grace" if one were so inclined.

Cineaste: Jasira's burgeoning sexuality becomes a flashpoint for all the adults in the story: her father Rifat is fearful of it and rigidly authoritarian as a re-sult—partly a reflection of his own Lebanese culture; Melina tries to help her understand the changes in her body, but is also a little fearful too; her mother's boyfriend Barry and Mr. Vuoso are attracted to it; her mother feels threatened by it. Is this "force field" her sexuality exerts a product of our own culture in which sexuality is so in the forefront—whether on billboards for escort services in the novel or in *Playboy* and other media in the film—excluding the Internet, of course, which is not yet a significant factor in the 1990 setting?

Ball: Just watch mainstream television and movies. Look at magazines. I cer-tainly believe that the idea and image of what a woman should be is so insanely sexualized, and so insanely packaged for consumption. It's starting to happen with men, as well, but I don't think young boys grow up thinking that their sexual attractiveness is their main source of self-esteem. It's just insane—it's really unhealthy and weird. And I think especially in suburbia, people may not be as exposed to more progressive points of view, the messages that shape their consciousness are what they get from TV, on billboards, in magazines—and from their immediate family, their role models. Jasira has two role models who are raging narcissists, who are made uncomfortable by her sexuality, and it's circumstances like these that create situations where things like this hap-pen—and they happen a lot. The statistics of child sexual abuse are shockingly high—a lot of adolescents have experienced situations similar to Jasira's. The prevailing cultural mythology in looking at child sexual assault is one that fetishizes victimhood—for women, for girls. For boys it's sometimes a little different—it's like, "Wow, you go, little stud!"

Cineaste: Interestingly, though, in the courts, female victims are less likely to be believed than are male victims—with many more prosecutions of offenders who have victimized boys than of those who have victimized girls.

Ball: That's very interesting—blaming the victim.

Cineaste: Especially if it's a woman.

Ball: Exactly. Another thing for which to thank our patriarchal society.

Cineaste: On a related topic, I feel the film somewhat shifts the point of emphasis on the issue of Jasira's virginity as compared with the novel, where it's presented from the adolescent perspective (almost playfully) as something Jasira and her friend Denise speculate about losing, to something more highly valued from an adult perspective in the film—especially in the climactic scene at Melina's where all the adults, and Thomas, seem preoccupied with Jasira's virginity until she reveals the truth about Mr. Vuoso. The scene was a little disturbing for me because it made me think of pre–sexual revolution days when a "good girl" was one whose virginity was intact.

Ball: I never really felt that Melina and her husband Gil were concerned about her virginity specifically, I just think they were concerned that she was so young and that she may have been having sex in their house right under their noses (when Jasira invites Thomas over after school)—and they were thinking, "How can we have let this happen? How can we have been so irresponsible?" Certainly, Rifat is a very old-world guy. He's going to want his daughter to remain a virgin her entire life. What I cut out of the book had to do with the question of how to fit this story into a movie. It was certainly not a conscious attempt to make virginity more—or less—an issue than it is in the book. It was more a sense of feeling that I couldn't really include all of the material with Denise because my first draft was 180 pages right off the bat. Some of my producers wanted me to cut Denise out of the movie entirely. Eventually I even had to cut forty-five minutes out of what I had originally shot. Any sense that there's a different kind of take on her virginity than in the book is completely unintentional.

Cineaste: You've said that you "wanted to capture the loneliness of the mundane" and the "disconnected confusion of middle-class existence" in *Towelhead*. While this seems an extension of a theme you were exploring in the screenplay for *American Beauty*, it takes on a very different resonance here, with the mélange of multiethnic characters and their complicated and often contradictory relationship to middle-class values and existence. Can you elaborate upon those differences a bit?

Ball: That was all in the book and I appreciated it because it felt like something I had never really grappled with before. I'm drawn to characters and stories that surprise me and force me to face my own limitations in how I see the world. I love the fact that Rifat is a Middle Eastern character and he's not Muslim—you immediately assume he is—but he's Catholic. He is totally on the American side of the war, in one sense. What I loved also is the fact that he loves his daughter so much but he's also so physically abusive. This suggests to me he was probably smacked around as a kid himself. Where did he learn this behavior? His character is encapsulated when he says of Mr. Vuoso, "This guy thinks I love Saddam—it's an insult. I'm an American citizen." When Jasira asks, "Did you tell him you don't?" and he responds, "I told him nothing, who is he to me?" I thought that was hilarious and it felt very real. I've known people like that.

In terms of middle-class values, I realize *Towelhead* is very similar to *American Beauty* in ways and that's probably a theme that really resonates with me, but again, it was all in the book—I didn't try to apply anything symbolic or thematic; it was organic to the material. And I have never intended these movies to represent all suburbia; I live in suburbia and I love it. I think if these movies were set in big cities, I doubt that people would see them as an indictment of urban living.

Cineaste: Rifat is both a racist, especially in regard to Jasira's African American boyfriend Thomas, and a victim of racism. It seems that his racist attitudes directed toward Thomas may have something to do with his own failed marriage to Gail, a blonde American woman.

Ball: I think his racism comes from having been the victim of racism himself. In the book, that's clearer. He's been called "towelhead" himself many times. When Gail married him, she was called "nigger lover." So it's a combination of the often-classic response of someone who's been victimized by racism being put in a position to victimize another group—the Hutus and the Tutsis jump to mind—and being shaped by a culture that places such a strong emphasis on pride, on family honor. When he says, "No one will respect you," he believes it. The concept of self-respect is less important to him.

Cineaste: Both the novel and the film are set in late 1990–early 1991 during the Gulf War, an event that, while not the central focus, is used as much more than a simple backdrop. It helps develop themes of racism, identity, and aspiration, especially in the case of Rifat living in a Houston suburb with an army reservist and racist as a next-door neighbor. Although there is some overt dialog about the war, mostly its presence is felt through the off-screen sounds of CNN coverage. How do you see the importance of the war to the film and the novel?

Ball: Another thing I loved about the book is that there was a war going on in the Middle East and there were people named Bush and Cheney calling the shots. I felt, wow, really not that much has changed. That's a big part of our culture—we want to be this colonial power in the world; we want to control other countries and their resources because we use something like 40 percent of the world's resources. This sort of schizophrenic schism that is right in the middle of many of the characters' lives leads them to do things that are not in their own best interest and becomes a microcosmic look at America and what America is now, what it's become in this post–Cold War hypersaturated media/marketing culture. It's not about anything that's real or that's natural.

Cineaste: We've talked about *American Beauty*, and I'm going to say something that's somewhat critical here—but in the context of your other work, which I very much admire. It strikes me that the characters and story of both *Towelhead* and your HBO series, *Six Feet Under*, are genuinely human and gently humorous, with three-dimensional characters engaging in the struggle of living and of dealing with conflicting emotions and desires. Yet the characters and situation of *American Beauty* strike me as rather mean-spirited, somewhat caricatured, and cynical, with a level of misogyny in the representation of the Annette Bening character—a kind of tone that I don't find present in your other work. Though not too many people share this opinion of *American Beauty*, I've wondered whether the finished film reflects what you had imagined when writing the screenplay or whether it may have moved in unanticipated directions.

Ball: I think you have a vision when you write something and that vision exists for you to get the words on the page, and then you let that go once it goes into production. I learned that lesson a long time ago, because filmmaking is such a hugely collaborative venture and other people are going to have better ideas than you did originally. *American Beauty* was an intensively personal screenplay for me to write; it was fueled by a lot of rage, so maybe that's what you're experiencing as mean-spiritedness.

I don't believe *Six Feet Under* or *Towelhead* are as fueled by rage, if at all. When I wrote *American Beauty*, as with everything I write, I felt a lot of compassion toward the characters. I'm interested in whacked behavior, but I'm more interested in where that behavior comes from. It certainly was not my intention to be mean-spirited. And I certainly never meant for Carolyn Burnham to represent all women. She was one character—a deeply unhappy character and one of the film's truly tragic characters, along with Colonel Fitts.

Cineaste: It just strikes me as very different in tone from your more recent work.

Ball: Having been a playwright, I had come out to Hollywood when offered a job writing for sitcoms. I wrote for sitcoms that were pretty dismal and disposable, and I was so angry and hated what I had become, so maybe there's some self-loathing expressed in *American Beauty*. For me it was a huge step forward in discovering my voice. We adapt, we change over time, and one's voice changes, hopefully. I don't want to do the same thing over and over again.

Cineaste: When I look at your work, I'd say you seem drawn to both suburban subjects that create a kind of death-in-life existence and that you're drawn to the subject of death, itself, which lingers always around the margins of life— probably one of the most powerful elements of *Six Feet Under*, and possibly also present in *True Blood*, the HBO series you're currently shooting. Is there anything about you, your own preoccupations that attracts you to these kinds of stories? Perhaps a Southern Gothic impulse connected with your having grown up in the South?

Ball: No, I don't think it's that. I think it's actually that when I was thirteen years old, I was in a car accident. My sister was driving the car and she was killed. And basically, death became a part of my life that day. My placid suburban existence was wiped out in one instant. I still lived in the same house, but the house was now filled with ghosts—not only my sister's. Both my parents were sort of hollowed-out, shell-shocked versions of the people they had been before. It eventually changed, of course, everything does, but death is still a constant companion of mine. For a long time, I tried to pretend it didn't exist, but then as I got older, I grew to welcome it. It's there, it's going to happen to all of us, and it's what defines life. We live in a culture that wants to deny mortality in a huge way. That experience when I was thirteen was definitely an initiation into a deeper sense of life than I had before.

Cineaste: That situation must have been very, very difficult for you, and it happened at a crucial time in your adolescence when so many other changes take place. Seeing your name on a tombstone during the opening-credits sequence of *Six Feet Under* initially struck me as a bit of sly black humor, and while it may be that, what you've just told me makes me think there's something a little bit more going on there.

Ball: My credit placement in the *Six Feet Under* title sequence was suggested by the company that designed the sequence, Digital Kitchen, and I thought it was sort of funny. Don't get me wrong, I'm not obsessed with death, I love living and I hope to live for a very long time. I just know that death is real and that no longer freaks me out.

Cineaste: You've worked in theater, television, and film. What does each one give you that the other doesn't? What lessons do you carry from one to the other?

Ball: Well, theater is more language-oriented—you can luxuriate in words, in rhythm, in the music and poetry of language. Film is like a dream—you can tell a story visually, with really beautiful images and symbols and subconscious currents and mythic moments. TV for me is like a novel because you can continue to develop a story over hours and hours and hours. You can really get to know the characters and be with them and grow with them in a way that you can't really do in film because in film you've got two hours—you've got to get there, to the resolution; there's this one issue the characters are dealing with, they deal with it, you get on the other side. A TV series can sprawl in ways that, for a writer, is very rich and nourishing and satisfying—well, for me at least.

A Big Messy Place: Alan Ball on *Towelhead*

K. J. DOUGHTON / 2008

From FilmThreat.com, Hamster Stampede LLC, September 9, 2008. Reprinted by permission.

Towelhead, the complex and audacious film from director Alan Ball, is already inciting anger, winning over enthusiasts, and prompting debate—even prior to its release. The Council on American-Islam Relations (CAIR) recently asked Warner Bros. and Warner Independent Pictures to change its volatile title. The film's creators and studio refused. Ball and author Alicia Erian, who wrote the 2005 novel on which *Towelhead* is based, released thoughtful yet assertive statements explaining why they stand by the controversial name.

The title, however, is but one aspect of the heated hullabaloo surrounding *Towelhead*. The tolerant folks at Fox News declared it the "feel-awful movie of 2007" after a Toronto Film Festival screening last year, denouncing the film's treatment of hot-button themes like statutory rape, teen sex, and racism.

But wait a minute. Does a film's acknowledging that bad things happen imply that it's condoning those bad things? I would challenge this mindset.

Like 1999's *American Beauty*, for which Ball won a Best Screenplay Oscar, *Towelhead* certainly boasts some repugnant, squirm-inducing moments. However, it balances these with scenes of comforting emotional truth. Tracing its young heroine's emotional journey from victim to survivor, the film deals with prickly adolescent themes in a shockingly honest manner. It tackles taboos with brave insight, but never condones the abusive, boundary-crossing behaviors of its messed-up characters. It's also pretty funny.

Ultimately, if you can wade through its unsettling early scenes, *Towelhead* offers an inspiring, unforgettable cinematic experience. In fact, the painfully uncomfortable initial passages enhance its final redemption (I was reminded of *The Color Purple*). Symbolizing relief, survival, and rebirth for its young protagonist, the film's last sequence hauntingly completes something larger and more hopeful than the sum of its parts. There's retribution at the end of Ball's emotional wringer.

Many associate Ball with his scripting prowess—and for good reason. After penning several episodes of mid-nineties sitcoms *Grace Under Fire, Cybill,* and *Oh, Grow Up,* he scribed *American Beauty.* Ball pocketed prestigious Oscar clout from that celebrated film, then continued his distinctive hybrid of storytelling with the cable series *Six Feet Under* (2001–2005). While writing and executive producing this hearse-black look at a Pasadena funeral home, the triple-threat occasionally stepped up to director's plate as well.

Towelhead, however, is Ball's first full-fledged foray into feature film direction. It's also an uncharacteristic spin on someone else's work. Erian's novel, which follows a thirteen-year old Lebanese-American girl navigating through a fog of cultural and sexual confusion, is a perfect match for Ball's artistic sensibility. This canvas of characters might have originated in someone else's noggin, but Ball uses *Towelhead* to continue exploring the superficial veneer of suburban America first mined in *American Beauty.* It's a landscape where, as he's fond of saying, "People are more than what they seem" (an observation that might also fit the telepaths and vampires inhabiting *True Blood,* Ball's upcoming HBO series).

Jasira (Summer Bishil) lives a life of pure teenage hell, walking on eggshells through the culturally volatile minefields of a sterile cul-de-sac and prison-like high school. At home, she's a scapegoat for every conflict created by Rifat, her sensationally pompous Lebanese father (Peter Macdissi)—a racist with Madonna-Whore attitudes towards women. Complicating matters further, Jasira is the target of desire for both a misguided, impulsive Army Reservist neighbor (Aaron Eckhart) and a hormone-driven, African American classmate (Eugene Jones). And her mother (Maria Bello)? Don't even get me started. Fortunately, an observant, perceptive couple played by Toni Collette and Matt Letscher also inhabits this troubled neighborhood.

Jasira endures both physical and sexual abuse, while acknowledging burgeoning womanhood with both fear and anticipation. Strong stuff? Sure. But Ball never exploits his actress or subject matter for cheap thrills. *Towelhead* isn't so much about Jasira's abuse as about how she overcomes it. Ball is clearly in her corner, empathic to the racial and sexual tensions she must negotiate.

But wait a minute. This is supposed to be a *comedy*?

Indeed—but from that uncomfortable, unforced school of organic, "laugh or cry" comedy. Macdissi plays Rifat as a self-involved jerk, but he's also a *funny* self-involved jerk. He denounces Jasira for not wearing "proper clothes." Later, the egomaniacal patriarch proudly brings home a trophy date whose attire is far more garish and slinky than anything found in Jasira's relatively tame wardrobe. Rifat is desperate to keep up with the Joneses, frantically erecting a flag in the front lawn (*Towelhead* is set during the Gulf War nineties)—not for the sake of patriotism, but because a next-door neighbor has done the same. We chuckle to keep from gagging.

The very thing that makes *Towelhead* unforgettable is also that which will ruffle feathers of more conservative viewers. A Lebanese immigrant who's Christian, and not Muslim? A thirteen-year-old girl who openly enjoys the inappropriate attention bestowed upon her by older men? A pedophilic National Guard Reservist who—after impulsive, reprehensible transgressions—follows through with a truly heroic gesture? These are not comfortable, cookie-cutter stereotypes. They're multi-layered, complicated creations. It's much easier to paint people with black and white brushstrokes. Clearly, however, Ball is not one to play it safe. Neither do his actors. In a fascinating zeitgeist of timing, Aaron Eckhart plays Mr. Vuoso, the Army Reservist pedophile. He's certainly a sick, troubled creature, but thanks to Eckhart's complex performance, not entirely unsympathetic. Even so, Vuoso is light years down the moral food chain from Eckhart's portrayal of ruined *Dark Night* hero Harvey Dent, who personified Gotham's heroic backbone until late into that blockbuster film. It will be interesting to see how multiplex-haunting Batman fans respond to Eckhart's contrasting turn in *Towelhead*, playing a much less likable character.

Finally, there's the film's emotionally stirring wrap-up, which suggests Jasira's escape from the twisted, nearly unbearable web of dysfunction she's been trapped in for the past two hours of celluloid. During a screening of *Towelhead* at this year's Seattle International Film Festival, these powerful closing passages moved me to unexpected, impossible-to-articulate tears. My prediction is that for every angry theater walkout prompted by *Towelhead*, several new fans will find validation and connection in this unique adolescent survival story.

A few days after screening *Towelhead*, I'm sitting across from Ball during a festival press interview. Dressed casually in jeans and denim shirt, the filmmaker shakes my hand and remarks, "It's a pleasure." Ball's appearance—brown hair, medium build—is that of a low-key everyman. But you'll take notice when he's in the room. Ball's charisma manifests itself through his warm, commanding voice and intense, articulate delivery. When I describe my emotional response to *Towelhead*, and ask for his analysis, Ball provides an immediate, dead-on interpretation. He's also not shy about pondering the messiness of the human psyche, society's discomfort with female sexuality, and the building of complex characters.

Doughton: You're known for an ability to create complicated, "five-dimensional" characters. What's your creative process for building a character? When are you happy with the way the character is finished? Is there a moment in which you say, "Okay—I've got it"?

Ball: Well, I can't really claim credit for building the characters in this movie, because they were already built by the author of the book. They are even more complex and multifaceted in the book. I think when I read the book, I certainly responded to how "five dimensional" the characters were. I just tried to keep that in my adaptation. It wasn't that hard, because I basically just had to transcribe a lot of things from the book and pick and choose what to keep and what to lose. So I don't really have a process, in terms of reaching a point where I go, "Okay, this character is complicated enough." I think when I create characters on my own, I'm a very instinctive writer, and I'm always drawn to the moments that are surprising. If I write a scene that feels conventional, then I feel like I'm not digging as deep as I can. And I'm not interested in seeing those conventional scenes or characters, because I've seen so many of them. If the character surprises me—once the surprise takes place and I can sort of understand where it came from—then I'm happy.

Doughton: If the character breaks away from the convention of what you would typically see . . .

Ball: Yeah—and if it tells you something about the character. For example, when I wrote *American Beauty*, in that scene where Annette Bening's character doesn't sell the house and starts slapping herself, that happened in a very organic way. I was going, "Oh, my God! This is crazy!" Then I realized that this tells you everything you need to know about her childhood.

Doughton: In that one moment . . .

Ball: Yeah! In that one moment. For me, that totally redeems all of her superficial, shallow behavior, because she was so traumatized as a child.

Doughton: There's a magic little moment in *Towelhead* that takes people by surprise, when Gil (Matt Letscher) suddenly speaks Arabic . . .

Ball: What I loved about the book is . . . people are more than they seem. There's a reason he speaks Arabic—he was in the Peace Corps, in Yemen, and he learned to speak Arabic then. But you don't expect this white suburban guy in Texas to be speaking Arabic. A lot of people who have written about the movie assume that Rifat is Muslim, because he's Middle Eastern. He's not. He's Christian. It couldn't be clearer. There's a Virgin Mary on the dashboard of his car. He'll genuflect before dinner. Jasira comes out and says it: "My dad's a Christian, just like everybody else in Texas." I'm always drawn to characters in movies or television shows or novels who are more than what they seem. They force me to confront my own stereotypes.

Doughton: This movie and *American Beauty* explored the veneer of suburbia, where all the hedges are immaculately cut, the lawns are perfectly mowed, and the houses all look the same. Everything on the surface should be in its place, prim and proper. Beneath, however, are these neuroses and obsessions and things that really aren't neat and tidy.

Ball: I don't think we're a neat and tidy species. I think the human psyche is a big, messy place. Somewhere along the line, we started believing that we should keep that mess hidden. I'm not advocating everyone becoming a sociopath or psychopath, or becoming pure id, but I do feel like there's a lot of self-loathing that we impose on ourselves by believing that we need to be perfect. By placing so much emphasis on the image that we present to others, and worrying so much about what other people think of us. I think a lot of lot of pathology comes from that sort of disconnect. It's not authentic.

Doughton: Kind of like the scene in which Rifat is redoing his garden, so that when Jasira's mother comes to visit, he will not be one-upped.
Ball: Absolutely. Not because he loves gardening. Not because he wants these flowers. It's like, "I'm gonna show her." That's what the flags are. These guys are not really patriots. They're trying to one-up each other.

Doughton: There were several moments in the film that showed Jasira asserting herself. It seemed like those scenes accented different points in the movie—key points in which she stands up for herself.
Ball: Yeah. I mean, ultimately, you're leading up to that moment where she says she will not return home with her father. It's hard for her to say, because she loves her father, and she knows he loves her in his way, as much as a narcissist can love anybody who is not them. It's all leading up to that moment where she really sort of accepts responsibility for herself, saying, "I'm gonna take care of myself. I'm the most important person now. I'm not gonna try to make you feel better." Alicia's book is so beautifully constructed, and the characters are so flesh and blood and completely alive. All of those moments came from the book. There are very few moments that I created on my own. I can't really claim credit. I just have to go, "Alicia did that and I just transcribed it." (Laughter)

Doughton: I understand that at one point, Alicia came onto the set and was startled by Macdissi's appearance . . .
Ball: Yes. His manner, and the way he looked, reminded her of her own father. It freaked her out a little bit, and made her uncomfortable.

Doughton: Not having read the book, I'm assuming that there were autobiographical elements in the story.
Ball: Certainly, the characters of the parents contain autobiographical elements. Her father's Egyptian. She did go to live with him in Texas at one point when she was young. Both her and her brother went. I had seen pictures of her father, and actually gave them to the hairstylists and costumers, because he looked so great. I said, "You should make him look like this guy as much as you can." And it sort of looks like Saddam Hussein, which is so funny.

Doughton: He has that great line about being both for the Gulf War and against it . . .

Ball: "I'm supporting one aspect of the war and protesting another aspect. It's the mark of intelligence—the ability to hold two conflicting ideas in your head at the same time." (Laughter)

Doughton: Can you describe some production hurdles with regard to getting a challenging subject like this made? I'm sure the subject matter made some people squeamish . . .

Ball: All the studios passed. Every single studio passed. A lot of people said, "I can't possibly make this movie. I have daughters." I sort of felt like, well, that's exactly why you should make this movie. But, whatever. We had to find independent financing, so there was that hurdle. There was the hurdle of casting Jasira, because it's not like there's a huge talent pool of Middle Eastern–looking actresses who can carry a movie who are eighteen but look thirteen. The Bond Company insisted that the actors playing Thomas and Jasira both be eighteen. Then, there was the selling of the movie, and getting it into film festivals. Some festivals passed, and some people didn't like it. Getting it to Toronto, Warner Independent bought it. After Warner Independent bought it, Warner Independent went away.

It's been a complicated road, but I don't think it's been a difficult road. I have to look at the fact that this movie got made, and the fact that Summer walked in. There was the actress to play this role. I believe everything happens for a reason. I can personally feel like studios should be banking more movies like this, but they're not gonna do it until a movie like this is successful. Look at what's successful. *Pirates of the Caribbean. Lord of the Rings. Batman. Indiana Jones.* Those are the movies that have made so much money. I think it's conservative of the studios to not try to make movies for adults, and to focus so many of their resources on making movies for teenage boys. But I can't blame them, from an economic standpoint.

Doughton: This film deals with certain mundane aspects of life, like inserting a tampon. But you don't see them very often in the movies. You watch *Towelhead*, and say, "Oh my God—when is the last time I saw a tampon in a movie?"

Ball: You know, I have to salute Seattle, because the response to the scene when the father holds up the tampon was the most subtle. I've been in screenings where people are like, "Oh, my God!" I've had writers accuse me of putting that in the movie intentionally to shock people. I personally don't find it shocking. I think it's biology. We all have mothers, and wives, and sisters, and daughters, and girlfriends—I mean, hello! The majority of the people on the planet deal with this, and yet it's considered so shocking.

Doughton: Ironically, horror films have come back with a vengeance. The *Saw* franchise made a lot of money. People are inundated with images of beheadings, mutilations, and gougings.

Ball: We are much more comfortable with violence than we are with sexuality, especially female sexuality. We are a patriarchal culture, and female sexuality is pretty terrifying. The fact that I go to screenings of this movie with smart, urban, educated people, and they still gasp at the site of a tampon, is hilarious to me. Hats off to Seattle for not being so squeamish. I know the movie is going to make a lot of people uncomfortable. But if I'd made a movie about a thirteen-year-old girl who was kidnapped and tortured, I don't think that anybody would bat an eye. And I think that's really twisted.

Doughton: What's your philosophy as to why one image is considered okay, but the other is not?

Ball: Because it's a male-dominated culture, and men are terrified of feminine sexuality because it is a power that is greater than any they will ever have. Violence and competition is kind of the basis for capitalism, so I think we're okay with that. Working together and coming together and being mutually supportive and not making yourself the most important, is considered kind of revolutionary. It goes against everything that we hold dear (laughs). Which is kind of insane, but . . .

Doughton: You have won an Oscar for *American Beauty*, and Emmys for *Six Feet Under*. How much does that boost your confidence, and your feeling that you can take on this very controversial film that some people are going to perceive the wrong way? Does that acknowledgment play into your willingness to take on a project like this, or is that totally irrelevant?

Ball: No, it's not irrelevant. I think that kind of validation does affect your confidence, of course. It certainly also affects the way people respond to you. You've been validated by this particular statue, or this particular organization, and people take what you say seriously. I developed a television show for ABC before I won the Oscar. Every single decision I made and every single idea I had was questioned, and eventually changed. Because that's what they do. They change things. Ultimately, the show turned out to be a show that I wouldn't even watch. After I won the Oscar, I wrote the pilot for *Six Feet Under* and took it to HBO. Granted, HBO is a different place. They actually want writers with strong points of view, and they don't really operate the same way that the traditional broadcast networks do. Everybody was like, "Well, what do you think?" For example, they said, "Who do you want to direct this?" I said, "I want to direct it." I think had I not won an Oscar, they would have said, "No. You don't have any experience." But because I won the Oscar, they were open to it.

In that sense, it certainly boosted my own confidence and gave me a sense of validation that is nice to have. At the same time, it's ultimately just—forget me for getting a little touchy feely here—but in spiritual terms, and terms of what's really important, it's pretty meaningless. The work is what's important. There was a moment where I suddenly felt like, "Oh—the next thing I do has to be a spectacular thing, again!" I pretty quickly realized, "No—do not fall into that trap. You got this statue (Oscar) and this statue (Emmy). You can look at it as, well, I've done that. You don't ever have to do that again. Just do the work that you believe in, and don't worry about the results, or how other people are going to respond to it."

Doughton: As opposed to having to one-up that, in some way . . .
Ball: Absolutely. It's like those actors that start in a movie that grosses a hundred million dollars. All of a sudden, it becomes about how every movie they do after that point is gonna open. What's the numbers on the opening weekend? They forget they're actors. They start thinking of themselves as commodities. That's really tragic.

Doughton: It seems like it's so easy to buy into that, too. I recall turning on my computer one morning, and reading some Internet headline next to a picture of Tom Hanks that said something like, "He's fallen from the A List." His last movie didn't make as much money as previous Hanks films that shot through the stratosphere of the box-office, so the press is perceiving him as a failure.
Ball: Everybody falls from the A List. Nobody stays up there forever. Is it more important to stay at the top of the A List, or to do work that you really believe in, and care about? At a certain point, you have enough money. You don't have to make, whatever (amount of money). That's why I respect actors who basically just do the work that they care about and they believe in. That's why I respect Aaron Eckhart. He plays roles where he finds the psychology of the characters, and finds out what's human about them.

Doughton: Maria Bello as well. You wouldn't do that for the box office—some of the roles that she has taken.
Ball: And Toni (Collette), too. Especially when the majority of movies are now comic book movies targeted to teenagers. I'm very fortunate, in that I have achieved a level of success and I have some financial stability that I thought I would never, ever have. So I never have to worry about those things. That's a luxury.

Doughton: Another striking thing about this movie is the set design. The cul-de-sac was such a character in the movie. You're not moving around. There aren't elaborate sets in different countries, like *Mission: Impossible*. How important was that setting to the film?

Ball: I always thought that it needed to be a fairly sterile environment. Her home, her neighborhood, her school. I wanted it to all be fairly . . . cold. You know what I mean? Not really warm or nurturing. Kind of institutional. There was a great show at one of the big museums—I think it might have been the Museum of Modern Art, but I'm not sure—years ago, called "The Pleasures and Terrors of Domestic Comfort." I got the catalog of that show. When I started thinking about the look of this movie, I went over all these (images) with the production designer, James Chinlund, who is really gifted. We wanted to see the electric cords coming out of the wall, and all of the vents. When we were sound mixing the movie, whenever the doors opened it was kind of like a pneumatic thing. There are these closed, air-conditioned environments that you can feel. It's like an air lock, almost.

Doughton: Very controlled . . .

Ball: Yeah. Very artificial, and sanitized, and cleaned up. Because that's also something about female sexuality. Women have to be controlled, and sanitized, and shaved, and made up. It was an architectural extension of that. William Eggleston was one of the photographers we really responded to.

And then at the same time, working with Tom Sigel, the cinematographer . . . you know, the story has mythic elements. From a sort of Joseph Campbell viewpoint, there's kind of a call to adventure, with the magazines. She really descends into an underworld, and is reborn at the end. Literally, when you see that baby. By having the architectural elements be very cold, we would be shooting in a way that was really warm, almost like a fairy tale. In a way, it is like a fairy tale. You look at the symbology of *Little Red Riding Hood*, it's exactly the same story. So . . . I hope I answered your question, sort of (laughter).

Doughton: You did. There was that sterility, in both the cul-de-sac, and the school.

Ball: The school's like a prison. I saw that school, and was like, "Oh, that's great!"

Doughton: Some of the most influential movies of our time have been about young people in perilous situations. These are roles that are hard for people to digest. There will be people who say, "I'm a father and I'm mad that a young actress has to be put through that." How would you respond to that?

Ball: Nobody forced her. I mean, it's a great role. It's one of the greatest roles that an actress could get in her entire lifetime. She was eighteen. Her mother was on the set every day. And the story we're telling is I think really important, in trying to shed light on how these things actually happen.

Doughton: And statistically, they do happen.

Ball: They happen a lot. Hello. We live in a culture where pornography is a big commodity. I bet you a lot of those girls are eighteen. I mean, open up *Playboy*. Those girls are like nineteen, twenty. Let's not kid ourselves. That's what I would say. And I would say, if you are the father of a young daughter, you talk to her, and you let her know that she can come to you with anything. And that she doesn't need to be ashamed of her body, or afraid to talk to you about those things. That's what you need to do. Don't get mad at me.

Doughton: Why do you think a guy like me would well up at the end of this movie? I'm still trying to work this out (laughter).

Ball: You know what? Because you are expecting her to be destroyed. You're expecting her not to bounce back. The fact that her life is taking a big turn for the better, and that there is hope, and that she's not destroyed by this process, is really moving. The conventional mythology is that she's damaged goods.

Doughton: But in a sense, she came out of this . . .

Ball: Stronger. And in control of her own body and destiny. She's gonna be taken care of and parented by people who really know how to do it. Her whole life is ahead of her.

Fresh Air Interview with Alan Ball: Talking *True Blood* and *Towelhead*

TERRY GROSS / 2008

From *Fresh Air*, NPR, September 10, 2008. Interview reproduced with permission of WHYY, Inc.

Gross: This is *Fresh Air*. I'm Terry Gross. After creating the HBO series *Six Feet Under* about a family that runs a funeral home and is steeped in death, Alan Ball has created a new HBO series about the undead. *True Blood*, which premiered on Sunday, is about vampires who have returned from the grave and live on a newly developed synthetic blood called TruBlood. Their presence is so new no one knows what to make of these vampires. Some people find them sexy; many people fear them. Some are just curious. The vampires have formed their own lobby group, which is pushing for a passage of a vampire rights act. The series is based on Charlaine Harris's Southern Vampire series of novels. Alan Ball also directed and wrote the new movie *Towelhead*, which we'll talk about a little later. Ball won an Oscar for his screenplay *American Beauty*.

Let's start with a scene from the first episode of *True Blood*. Anna Paquin plays a waitress in a small Louisiana town. A handsome, mysterious stranger has just walked in, and she's ready to take his order.

(Soundbite of *True Blood*)

Alan Ball, welcome back to *Fresh Air*. Let's start with some of the basic plot points for *True Blood*. Why have the vampires come out of their coffins and returned?

Ball: The vampires have made their presence known to humans because there's been a development of synthetic blood by a Japanese biotech firm for medical purposes, which the vampires claim satisfies all their nutritional requirements, and so there's no reason for humans to fear them. And they've put together a lobbying organization and they're lobbying for equal rights, and ultimately what is at the root of everything, which is not very clear at this point in the show, is they want ownership. They want to be able to own things. And whether or not vampires can actually survive on TruBlood alone is also something we just sort of have to take their word for. Although in this world there are plenty of people who are willing to let vampires feed on them.

Gross: Yeah, because it's kind of a kick for people. It's like, wow, they're vampires.
Ball: It's a kick. It usually is accompanied by sex, and apparently vampires are pretty good at sex . . .

Gross: Where does that come from? Where does that part of the lore come from?
Ball: Well, you know, I wondered about that, and I think—well, certainly if you've been around a hundred years, you have time to perfect your technique. But I also think—and part of the way we're playing vampires and the supernatural in general is that it's not something that exists outside of nature. It's actually a deeper, more primal manifestation of nature, so deep and primal sometimes that we as humans don't even have the perception to see it or feel it. So those are my own answers to the questions. In the books that the series is based on, the Southern Vampire series by Charlaine Harris, pretty much all the vampires seem to be excellent bedfellows.

Gross: You know, it's funny, in the original Bram Stoker *Dracula* novel, the novel seems to be so much about sexual fear, you know, sexual attraction, sexual fear. And it's almost like a metaphor for sexually transmitted disease.
Ball: Well, I think, also, it certainly took on that characteristics once the AIDS epidemic hit. But it's also just a metaphor for sex. You know, somebody is penetrated, bodily fluids are exchanged. There is a sort of surrender, so it's a pretty potent—no pun intended—metaphor for just sex in and of itself, I think, and has been ever since Bram Stoker's *Dracula*.

Gross: And in your series, *True Blood*, there's a big connection between sex and danger, and there's several characters in it who really like sex and danger combined. And sometimes it gets more dangerous than they expected. But why was that interesting for you, exploring that connection that exists for some people?
Ball: I don't really know. I think it was just a visceral thing. I think when I started reading the books, they had a sort of pulp-y sensibility. Everything was heightened, and each chapter ended with a cliffhanger, and there's a big body count, and danger lurks around every corner, as does romance, as does finding someone you love or meeting your maker . . . however you choose to interpret that. And there was such a fun, thrill-ride adventure, science fiction, if you will, feeling to the books that I just sort of went with that. It felt really

liberating to me after working so long on material that was basically just about the intricacies of humans relating to each other to actually go into a world where just fantastic things happen, and it's just kind of fun and silly. And when I pitched it to HBO for the first time I said, "This is popcorn television. You know, this is a popcorn TV show."

Gross: What else did you tell them?

Ball: Well, they asked me, "Well, what is the show about?" And I had no answer. But being the Hollywood person that I have become in some ways, unfortunately over the years, I just started talking and hoped that something would come out of my mouth that sounded vaguely coherent. I think I talked about the fears that we project onto any minority group that is misunderstood or feared, and then I said, "At the heart of it, though, it is a show about the terrors of intimacy." And I heard myself say that and I thought, well, that sounds pretty good. And actually the more that I look at it, I can sort of see that it is, in a sense, about the terrors of intimacy, about breaking that wall that keeps you separate and safe from a sometimes savage and dangerous world; and letting another person in, ultimately, is a terrifying act.

Gross: Especially when you're just meeting the person and you don't really know who they are. And, you know, in a metaphorical way it's done in *True Blood* because the main female character is telepathic. She can read people's minds, but not the mind of the vampire that she's fallen in love with. And so in this character, she's meeting this vampire and not really sure, like is he good or evil or a combination of both, or can she trust him or not? And . . .

Ball: But at the same time, she can relax and just be herself without putting up this guard that she has to work at and . . .

Gross: Yes, she guards against other people because reading their minds . . .

Ball: She doesn't want to hear other people's thought.

Gross: . . . really complicates things. Yes.

Ball: Yeah.

Gross: They're usually not good thoughts.

Ball: And it's a really sort of seductive space for her to just relax like that.

Gross: My guest is Alan Ball, and his new series *True Blood* just premiered on HBO, and it's about vampires who come out of their graves because synthetic blood is now available so they no longer have to feed on humans. Did you grow up with any vampire movies or books?

Ball: You know, when I was a kid, *Dark Shadows* started airing, and me and some of the neighborhood kids would rush home from school so that we could be there when it started. And when that organ music came on or whatever the music was—it was kind of spooky and there were shots of waves crashing against rocks—we would hold our necks like we couldn't breathe while the music was on. And then once the music was over, we'd leave and go outside and play because the show itself was kind of boring to us. But that was—I mean, I knew what vampires were, but I've never really—I'm not what one would call a vampire aficionado. I haven't read a lot of the popular vampire fiction. There are movies and television shows I've never even seen.

Gross: Have you seen the Bela Lugosi *Dracula* or . . .
Ball: Yes, of course I've seen that.
Gross: *Nosferatu*, the Klaus Kinski *Nosferatu*?
Ball: I have seen the Klaus Kinski *Nosferatu*.

Gross: In the Klaus Kinski *Nosferatu*, there's so much brooding about the curse of eternal life. People think they'd love to live eternally, but if you ask the Klaus Kinski Nosferatu, he would see it as a curse.
Ball: Yeah, I would imagine that there is a curse aspect to it, because if you live forever, then why is this day important? You know, you lose everything. Everything you have you lose eventually, unless there are other vampires. And I don't know, I just feel like the finite nature of life is kind of what makes it important.

Gross: You had to think a lot about blood in making this, both how you wanted—like what kind of stage blood you wanted to use, what color it should be, what thickness it should be. You had to think about how it should taste to people, so what kind of things did you do blood-wise to prepare for making *True Blood*?
Ball: Well, in the world of *True Blood*, there is human blood and there's vampire blood. Human blood is the blood that flows through all of our veins. It's the same color, it's the same thickness, it's the same viscosity. Vampire blood is a highly volatile, organic substance that, when ingested by humans, can have aphrodisiac qualities. It can have increased strength, increased senses. As a byproduct, it can also be hallucinogenic. It can be a doorway into other perceptions. And so we wanted to make that very different and very sort of really decadent, so we made it darker and thicker. It's almost like molasses, and it's a really dark brownish red.

As far as what it tastes like, I never really even thought of that. We certainly have—I just let the actors act, you know, how they seem to enjoy it when they start drinking it, and we have dialogue referring to how TruBlood, the synthetic blood, is a poor substitute for refined vampire palates.

Gross: I'd love to hear what casting was like, how people showed up, especially for the lead vampire role, the role that Steve Moyer plays. How do people show

up for the role? Were they wearing what they thought would be appropriate?
Ball: A lot of people came in wearing all black. I've learned, now that I've done a season of the show, you've got to be careful when you give an actor fangs because their tendency is to go mad immediately and start doing vampire acting, which I really wanted to avoid. I didn't want to have any of the strange contact lenses that come into—you know, that all of a sudden their eyes change when their fangs come out, or there's any sort of prosthesis change in their facial structure. I just wanted to give them fangs and let them act.

It was a really hard role to cast. We saw a lot of men. There were people that I took to the network that the network was not crazy about. There were people the network wanted to see that I was not crazy about. And then Stephen, I saw off a video that a casting director in London had made and I watched it in a tiny little postage stamp–size video on my computer, and there was something so, for lack of a better word, real about him and the sort of world-weary but tragic feeling that he brought to it—aside from being really, really handsome, which helps.

Gross: In a worn-out way.
Ball: Yeah, exactly. Like he's been through hell. And there's actually a great line in one of the episodes where Sookie says, "How old are you?" and he said, "I was thirty human years when I was made vampire." And she goes, "Wow, you look older than that." And he says, "Well, life was harder then." But he really brought—for me what he brings to the role is the sense of, it's tragic. It's tragic what happened to him. He did not ask to be made vampire. He lost his family and his children, he lost his life. And now he's condemned to wandering the world at night, not being a part of the world that he was so much a part of before he was made vampire, before he went off to fight in the Civil War. So we brought Stephen over, and I worked with him for a day, and then we went into HBO, and it became very obvious very fast that this was the guy we'd been waiting for.

Gross: So did he not dress in all black for the audition?
Ball: You know, he wore jeans and a blazer.
Gross: No chains or anything?
Ball: No, he didn't come in in all black and he didn't come in with the sort of extreme eyebrows and that kind of thing. And I liked that about him, because I want Bill to just be a guy who is a vampire.

Gross: You said you wanted to just give your actors fangs and let them act.
Ball: Yeah.
Gross: So talk about the fangs.
Ball: Well, in keeping with our idea about the supernatural being a deeper,

more profound manifestation of nature, we really thought a lot about the physiology of the fangs, and we created fangs that actually lie flat along the roof of the mouth and then click into place when a vampire is in danger or aroused or ready to feed, much like a rattlesnake's fangs click into place. And we actually created a model of teeth—showing how the fangs click in and click out, and then we put the fangs, not with the four front teeth between them, but with only two, because it worked better for the physiology of the rattlesnake, the snake fang working, and I like that because it looks a little different. It doesn't look like the classic thing, and I like the fact it's not just like the supernatural teeth morph into fangs. You know, it's actually part of their physiology, and there's a sound they make when they click, which is kind of like a weapon being loaded. So it really worked. You know, it works well for the show in that regard, I think.

Gross: Did you have to work with a dentist in order to get them made?
Ball: Oh, yeah. And even when we cast a guest vampire for one episode, they have to go off and get impressions made of their teeth, and they make fangs. And it's hilarious to watch the dailies because the actors will make a face, and then we'll stop and everybody will go get their little plastic cup with their fangs and put their fangs in and make sure they fit, and then the scene keeps going.

Gross: So can the actors activate the fangs by pressing a button in their mouth?
Ball: No, no, no. They have to—that has to be done with visual effects. They actually—the fangs are just—the actual fangs that they place on their teeth once they've extended, but the extending and the retracting of fangs we have to do as a visual effect, and we have to put little dots on the actors' face as tracking marks

Gross: I see.
Ball: So if you ever watch an unfinished cut of our show, there's some unintentional humor in those moments.

Gross: So we talked a little bit about casting Stephen Moyer as the lead Vampire. Anna Paquin plays a waitress who is telepathic and starts to fall in love with the vampire and he with her, or at least that's the way it's looking. So, talk about why you cast her. People probably know her from *The Piano*.
Ball: And the *X-Men* movies.
Gross: And the *X-Men* movies, yeah. In *The Piano* she was, what . . .
Ball: Eleven.
Gross: Yeah, she was really young.
Ball: Yeah. When I heard that Anna wanted to come in and read for Sookie I was surprised. I thought, well, why does she want to do this? She's a movie star.

But she aggressively pursued it, and then I thought about it and I thought, well, it makes perfect sense. It's a great role. It's the lead of the show. She's sexy and she's a romantic heroine and she's strong and she gets to play the gamut of human emotion and also have all these great chase scenes and fight sequences. It actually makes perfect sense to me.

And I wasn't too sold on the idea at first, because Sookie is described in the books as being blond and blue-eyed, and I had only known Anna with dark hair, which is her natural hair color. But once she came in and she started reading and I started working with her, what she was playing and what I really thought made the character really interesting was I could see that this is a woman who had been hearing other people's thoughts her entire life. And that she was kind of skittish and nervous and jumpy and a little angry, and it kept her from being—you know, a lot of girls came in and they were like sorority girls. They overdid the Southern accent, or they came in dressed like Daisy Mae, and I sort of said, "Mm, no." And the character just came alive in a way with Anna that was the most interesting, and so that's who we cast.

Because I always feel like I will have a clear idea of what I think a character looks like when I write it, but the minute I start going into casting I let it go, because you want to be open to people coming in and doing different interpretations, because sometimes those interpretations are going to be better, and they're going to work better and they're going to make the character live more.

Gross: Alan Ball, you have a new movie that's about to premiere called *Towelhead*, and it's a movie about a thirteen-year-old girl who is the daughter of a Lebanese American father and American mother, but the parents are separated and the thirteen-year-old is now living with her mother and her mother's boyfriend. And the movie is really about her transition into being a sexual person and how confusing it is for her and for the people around her. Would you describe the opening scene?

Ball: The opening scene of *Towelhead* is very similar to the opening scene of *Towelhead* the novel in that Jasira's living with her mother and her mother's live-in boyfriend, Barry, who's a little bit younger than her mother, and is kind of a stoner and a nice guy. And Jasira has—girls have been making fun of her at school in swim class because her pubic hair can be seen around the edge of her bathing suit. So Barry offers to help her shave. And that's the opening scene of the movie. The mom finds out about this, flips out—understandably—and sends her daughter away to live with her father rather than kicking her boyfriend out.

Gross: And we should explain, when he shaves her, I mean, what we see is she's wearing her bathing suit and she has shaving cream around the periphery of the bathing suit so she could shave off the offending hair—

Ball: I've always thought that Barry was not—in his mind, I think he's not a very bright person and I think he probably smokes a lot of pot. I think he thinks he's doing her a favor. It's not like—I don't think he sexualizes her, but at the same time he knows to tell her, "It's probably best if you don't tell your mom about this."

Gross: So the mom decides to send her away, send Jasira away to live with her father. And I want to play a short scene. This is Maria Bello as the mother and Jasira is played by Summer Bishil, and they're both at the airport as the mother is saying goodbye and explaining why she has to send Jasira away, and Jasira is weeping.
(Soundbite of *Towelhead*)
Gross: That's a scene from Alan Ball's new movie *Towelhead*, and, boy, that's just about the worst thing that the mother could have said to the daughter there, to blame her for her own sexuality and for the effect that it has on men. And the mother takes no responsibility for what's happening in her own home.
Ball: Well, it's too threatening. It's too competitive. She's hyperaware of the fact that she's getting older, her daughter is attractive, her boyfriend's looking at it, and she's so terrified of being alone that the only way she can deal with it is to get rid of her daughter. Something she does grow to regret.

Gross: Your movie *Towelhead*, which you wrote and directed, is based on a novel, and I'm wondering what you related to about the story of a girl's confusing feelings about her own sexuality. The novel's written by a woman.
Ball: Right.
Gross: So tell me what you related to about the story.
Ball: I think what I related to in the story was how much I was able to understand Jasira and what she was feeling and her desire to feel some pleasure or some sense of power and adventure in what was basically a very sterile and arid life, in which everybody seemed to want to control her. Everybody seemed to want to keep her from doing anything. Everybody seemed to want to just deny her her very existence and for her to do the same thing.

Gross: Except for the men who want to take advantage of her.
Ball: Except for the men who want to take advantage of her, but even they don't really see her. They see an idea that fits into their own particular pathology. But they don't really see that there is an actual person there. So I guess what I related to, it felt so real. It felt so vivid and so true, and I loved the messiness of the feelings, and I loved the fact that the story refused to judge any of the characters; even though some of the characters do reprehensible things, the story refused to not see them as human beings. And I certainly responded to that.

I guess, you know, going back to my own youth, my own becoming aware of my own sexuality when I was thirteen, because I'm gay, there was a lot of shame and confusion and secrecy and it's like I'm not supposed to be feeling these things. I shouldn't be feeling these things. And so I guess there's a little bit of transference that I could get into her head and identify with her a little bit, but mostly it was just the sheer power of the writing and the power of the story and the fact that she goes on this harrowing journey, that she is somewhat provocative. She's curious, and once again the story refuses to condemn her for that. And ultimately she sort of transcends a horrible event in a way that makes you feel like she is really in control of her own body and her own identity and her own life for the first time.

And that to me felt very refreshing, because I feel like the conventional wisdom model that we have built so that we can wrap our brains around such a horrible event as child sexual assault is that the child is 100 percent innocent victim, is ruined for life, doesn't do anything to provoke, does not enjoy it in any way, is not curious, and the adult instigator is a subhuman, evil predator who has no soul, and it's the worst thing that a human being can be. I just feel like that denies both—that really keeps us from seeing a lot of what actually allows these events to happen, and, I don't know, I just felt it was so refreshing to see a young girl character, especially, experience something like this and not be destroyed by it. In fact, I feel like she was probably a little stronger because of it.

Gross: I guess I feel I should acknowledge here that for some people, they really are victims, and there are instances, a lot of them, where the guy really has behaved like a monster. The adult really has behaved . . .
Ball: Absolutely, and I'm not denying that at all. I just think that any time we try to simplify something into one paradigm, that what it does is it denies us from seeing a lot of the complexity. And considering that this is such an incredibly common experience, I do think there is a somewhat of a knee-jerk need in our culture to sort of fetishize victimhood and make it something in and of itself, which is not always good. That's just what I'm saying, but that's not to say that people who do this are not doing something monstrous.

Gross: This might be too personal so we'll just move on if it is, but I'll ask it and then you can tell me if you want to answer. When you were young, when you were, say, Jasira's age, thirteen, did you have an encounter with an adult man that was a very ambiguous encounter for you?
Ball: I did; not when I was thirteen. I was younger. I don't remember exactly how old I was. I did.
Gross: And—I don't know what you're comfortable talking about in terms of that event and how it affected you as a person and as an artist.
Ball: Well, I'm sure it affected me in a lot of ways. I'm sure it affected my

feelings about sexuality, my body, whatever. I don't see myself as a victim, and I'm not particularly interested in identifying with victimhood. That's why I don't even really think that I was molested. It was someone who was older, but he was not, you know, that much older. It wasn't like he was a grown, adult man. I don't know. I've certainly never talked about it, and it's not because I'm ashamed of it. It's just that it's like, well, that happened, you know. I feel like other things happened to me in my life that were way more traumatic and way more damaging that I have had to struggle with to sort of get past the trauma for years and years and years.

But I know a lot of people go, like, "What's with this guy? Why does he keep writing about old guys lusting after young girls? What a pervert, what a creep." And the reason I write about these things is because it has personal resonance for me.

Gross: Have you tried to figure out what was going on in this guy's mind when you were young and he had that encounter with you?

Ball: I think—no, I haven't.

Gross: I ask because you tried to get into, say, the Kevin Spacey character's mind in *American Beauty*.

Ball: Well, I think he was—I think growing up as we did in the South, and the mid-sixties probably, I think he was probably aware of homosexual feelings on his part and probably aware of a certain energy within me, and because we didn't live in a culture where there were really any sort of legitimized ways of exploring that, because at that point, you know, one didn't even talk about being gay or consider it as just another expression of human sexuality. I think probably because we were both so ashamed by just the cultural take on who and what we were that it, you know, it just sort of happened. My memories are very sketchy, and I don't want to—I mean, I'm fine to talk about this, but I don't want to be one of those people who say, "I was molested!"

Gross: Well, do you think of the word "molested," or do you think that's the wrong word for what you experienced?

Ball: No, I'm just talking about people who go on TV or go get interviewed by magazines and it's all about, "I'm sharing this deep painful secret." Because I sort of feel like, you know what? You want some painful secrets? I got much more painful secrets than that one.

Gross: You know, I'm curious. Like in *Towelhead*, the Jasira character, the thirteen-year-old, has somebody who enters her life who is a sane adult, like maybe for the first time there's a real, sexually sane adult in her life. Was there someone like that in your life who you could turn to when you were confused about your own sexual identity?

Ball: You know what? I think my sister would have served that role. I think my sister knew that there was something different about me. I remember she gave me a poster for my birthday once. It was that Thoreau quote about, "if a man marches to the beat of a different drummer." I think one of her close friends in high school was a guy who was gay. I think she would have been that person, but she died.

Gross: She died in a car accident, right?
Ball: Yeah, when I was thirteen. And then everybody in the family went insane after that. So I was really sort of on my own.
Gross: Right.
Ball: In a lot of ways like Jasira was. Now that you mention it, I can sort of see that, that sort of left alone in the house. You know, that sort of solitary existence where the adults are all off, in my case, dealing with their own breakdowns and that kind of thing. But I certainly related to that as well.

Gross: Do you think a lot of adults underestimate the sexual feelings of children and teenagers?
Ball: Yes. I think—actually one thing that was really interesting. When I sent the script out, a lot of people passed on it, a lot of people who ran studios, and literally I heard comments like, "I can't possible make this movie. I have daughters." And I thought, and that's exactly why you should make this movie. Yeah, I think people don't want to think that kids are sexually curious, but I think when we all just think back to our own childhood, of course we are. And especially in a culture now where everything is saturated with sex. Just watching mainstream TV or going to the movies or turning on your computer and looking at the images that are on your welcome page. It's just sex, sex, sex. And so I think it's much more in the faces of children now than it was when I was a kid, and I was fascinated by it. Yeah. I think kids are naturally curious about sex, and there's nothing wrong with that. They just need somebody to be straight with them.

Gross: During one of our interviews on *Fresh Air* about *Six Feet Under*, you talked about how you really found it very difficult to go to funerals, and you'd often try to find like an excuse not to go. In part because your sister died when you were thirteen and it was such a traumatic experience for you and your family that it was just very difficult to deal with funerals. And then of course you made *Six Feet Under* which is about a family that runs a funeral home. And as we talked about, your new series *True Blood* is about vampires, the undead, who have slept in coffins and there's graveyards in it and so on. I read that after *Six Feet Under* was completed your mother died.

Ball: Yes.

Gross: Did you have to prepare her funeral?

Ball: Yes.

Gross: Did she . . .

Ball: I mean, my brother did the bulk of the work, because he was there at the time and he had sort of assumed the role as primary caretaker, but I was definitely there for that. And I definitely went to the funeral and I definitely was there in the meetings with the people at the funeral home. And it was very funny, because my mom had left very specific wishes. She wanted the cheapest casket. She didn't want any obituaries. She wanted a funeral with only her immediate family. She was, like, "Don't do anything fussy." And, you know, those were her wishes, so I felt like we had to—we had no choice. We had to honor them.

Gross: Do you know why she wanted that?

Ball: I think part of it is just because she was always a person who really did not like people making a fuss over her or taking care of her. She was fiercely, fiercely independent. She was a child of the Depression, so she was really aware of money. You know, she didn't have any money. She didn't want to spend any money on something like a funeral. But while we were there at the funeral home, the young guy who worked there came up to me and said, "I just want you to know I'm in this business because of you." And I was really touched by that. I thought—at first, I said, "Well, that's a good thing, right? You like this business?" He said, "Oh, yeah. I love it. I'm so glad I found it." And then I was really touched by it.

And it was—it was hard. I mean, seeing your parent dead is hard. She was in this cheap casket and I wanted to look at her. We wanted to see her one last time, and so we looked at her and I kissed her, and that's something I never could have imagined myself doing.

Gross: Did she look like herself?

Ball: Not at all. No, she looked like something else. She refused to be embalmed. She did not want that, and she did not have anything, any sort of cosmetic or anything done. But just the way she was laying, gravity did something different to her face, so it really looked like somebody different. And, you know, with her spirit gone, it wasn't her.

Gross: I sometimes really miss the characters from *Six Feet Under*. Do you think about them much?

Ball: I don't. I feel like—when *Six Feet Under* ended, it felt to me as if it was the right time, and it was time to let them go. And I think in shooting that last episode, we all sort of grieved for them, so I've kind of let them go and I've said goodbye to them. But I love that they stay in your mind. That means that they were powerful on some level.

Gross: Well, Alan Ball, thank you so much for talking with us.
Ball: Thank you, Terry. I really love talking to you. Let's do it again.

Life and Death, Drama and Humor, Join Hands

KINNEY LITTLEFIELD / 2011

From *The Writer* 124, no. 8 (August 2011). Reprinted by permission of Kinney Littlefield.

Depicting the dark ironies of contemporary American life—that's what Alan Ball does best. An acclaimed writer for film and television since 1994, Ball has never shied from probing the interwoven pain and joy of existence, through complexly written characterizations and subtly shaded dialogue. Ball's Academy Award–winning screenplay for the 1999 feature film *American Beauty* was a searing ode to suburban family dysfunction. *American Beauty* earned lavish critical praise and snagged the Oscar for best motion picture that year. Subsequently, Ball's seminal HBO series, *Six Feet Under* (2001–2005), set in a Los Angeles funeral home, captured a whole mausoleum's worth of tragic-comic family trauma—and gave funerals a new kind of high-profile chic. More recently, Ball captured the bittersweet coming-of-age story of a Lebanese American girl in Houston, in his 2007 film, *Towelhead*, which he directed and adapted from the Alicia Erian novel.

Now, with his current hit vampire series, *True Blood*, in its fourth season on HBO, Ball continues to explore the intersections of life and death, love and hate, this time in Bon Temps, Louisiana, a small but undeniably otherworldly town. Adapted from Charlaine Harris's series of best-selling Southern Vampire novels, *True Blood* features mind-reading waitress Sookie Stackhouse (Anna Paquin) and her on-and-off-again lover, the courtly undead gent Bill Compton (Stephen Moyer), plus a clutch of other lethal creatures, human or not.

Seasoned storyteller that he is, Ball can trace his affinity for the precarious balance between life and death to a painfully personal place. When Ball was thirteen, he survived a car accident on his twenty-two-year-old sister's birthday. His sister was driving. Ball sat in the passenger seat and watched her die. If the ghost of that experience lingers, it informs Ball's skill at painting the pathos, humor, and horror of everyday life—which has earned him an armful of writing, directing, and producing awards and a devoted fan-following to boot.

Driven and prolific, Ball, fifty-four, lives in Los Angeles. He recently shared his writing savvy with us, and talked *True Blood*, *Six Feet Under*, and breaking into the writing biz.

Littlefield: How did you get your start in television?
Ball: A play I had written, called *Five Women Wearing the Same Dress*, got me a job offer to come to Los Angeles and write for *Grace Under Fire* [a 1993–98 comedy series on ABC] in 1994.

Littlefield: When you started writing for *Grace Under Fire*, did you have a mentor, someone who took you under their wing?
Ball: It was much more a matter of sink-or-swim. I was just thrown into the pool and I had to learn to swim pretty fast.

Littlefield: With *Six Feet Under*, how did you come up with a core premise, and how did you develop that into a script?
Ball: The premise for *Six Feet Under*—basically a family-run funeral home—was pitched to me by [entertainment president] Carolyn Strauss at HBO after *American Beauty* came out. At the time I was working on a show for ABC that I had created, a sitcom called *Oh, Grow Up*. And then a couple of months later ABC cancelled the series and I knew I didn't want to do another network sitcom. So I wrote a pilot for *Six Feet Under*, I just made it up. I did a little bit of research. I read the book *The American Way of Death*. I gave the pilot to HBO and they said "We like it. Let's make it."

Littlefield: How did you find the right balance between humor and drama on *Six Feet Under*, and how do you balance them on *True Blood*?
Ball: It's just instinctive. I find my own life is filled with tragedy and farce, and I don't really think of them as being that separate. I've experienced a lot of really tragic things in my life.

At the same time I feel my sense of humor has helped me survive. That's just a very organic place that I come from. My own outlook on life is that drama and humor coexist. Death is a part of life. We can pretend that it isn't, but it is. Eventually that illusion is going to get shattered.

Littlefield: When you were dealing with issues of death in *Six Feet Under*, did you find it difficult to write because the material was so emotional?
Ball: I'm always very much aware that this is fiction. These are not real people. That being said, when I wrote the final episode of *Six Feet Under*, it was very emotional and I cried. I think that was partially because I was grieving the end of the show. It was the end of these characters and their world.

In a way *Six Feet Under* was like therapy for me. It was my way of making peace with grief because I've lost a lot of people in my life. Now it's still incredibly painful, but there's not that panic that I used to have. Now I know grief is a part of life and it's necessary. It's the price of love. And we will lose everything, eventually—including ourselves.

Littlefield: How does your writing process work on *True Blood*?

Ball: I work with five other writers, so it's a total of six writers. It's very collaborative. We outline stories as a group, we break stories—figure out the plot, figure out exactly what happens in each episode—as a group. We start by looking at the season as a whole, and we say, "OK, what is Sookie's story throughout the season and what is Bill's story throughout the season?" Then we figure out what the three or four "beats" [parts of the story] are for each character and we order how they'll play out in an episode and how they'll interweave with each other.

One writer will go off and write that script, and then they'll come back in and we all read it and we give notes as a group. A lot of times the notes are, "That doesn't sound like a word that Sookie would use," or "This doesn't really feel like Sam's [shape-shifter Sam Merlotte, played by Sam Trammell] voice."

Littlefield: How do you decide which episodes of *True Blood* you will write yourself?

Ball: It works out well for me to write two episodes a year. I take the ones that nobody else wants. That's my job. As we're breaking stories, people say, "I really respond to this one," "This story really means a lot to me," or "I need to do episode four because I'm getting married and I want to be able to plan my wedding." It's a mixture of things. I'm going to be working around the clock from the beginning of prep [preproduction] to the end of post [postproduction] so it doesn't matter to me. If the other writers want an episode strongly, that's means they're going to do a really good job. They're going to be personally invested in it.

Littlefield: How do you determine how much growth or change your characters will go through each season on *True Blood*?

Ball: Each season is a book in the series of novels written by Charlaine Harris. So we have source material that we can start from. And I never start out and go, "OK, Sookie needs to have seven big moments this season."

One difference between *True Blood* and *Six Feet Under* is that *True Blood* has developed organically into a show that has in every episode at least one, maybe more, of what I call "what the f—" moments, where it's like, "Wow, I've never seen that before, that's really shocking, I didn't see that one coming." But we try to make sure that everything evolves out of a character's emotional life or challenges a part of their character, so it's not just a random event happening.

And as the show goes on, the mythology within the show grows, and you have to be true to it. You can't just say, "OK, so now this happens because it would be cool." You have to remain true to the world and the laws that you've set up.

And the story has to grow out of the characters. When I was growing up I would watch a lot of TV shows where characters were basically chess pieces on a board that could get moved around to serve any story, whether it made sense emotionally or not. [On *True Blood*] we tend to come from a very character-based place when we break our stories.

Littlefield: Are there any benefits or drawbacks to adapting material from novels to television?
Ball: I can't think of any drawbacks. I mean, there's only so much one person can think of. At some point you have to start working with other sources, or collaborating with other people, because otherwise you're just going to start repeating your own personal mythology over and over again.

Littlefield: How much attention do you pay to Charlaine Harris's fanatical fan base—and *True Blood*'s?
Ball: I would never change things on the show because of the way somebody responded to it on the Internet. It's not my job to fulfill people's expectations. It's my job to tell the best story that I know how to tell. People are clamoring for Sookie and Eric [a powerful vampire] to get together. The minute that happens—if it happens—they're going to be clamoring for Sookie to get back with Bill. I don't pay much attention to it. There are writers on my staff who do pay attention to this, and they let me know.

Littlefield: What, to you, is really good writing for television?
Ball: It's complicated characters—I'm not a big fan of heroes or perfect people. I also like stories that surprise me, that don't go where I thought they were going to go. Good writing is not just craft. It involves some level of emotional investment. You have to care about the characters, you have to be empathetic. That's the genius of *Breaking Bad*, *Dexter*, and *Mad Men*. The characters at their centers are doing really bad things—and yet I still care about these people.

Littlefield: How does TV writing compare to feature film writing?
Ball: TV writing is light years ahead of feature film writing right now. When you have twelve episodes, twelve hours, to tell a story—as opposed to two hours—you can be more complex in depicting how people rise or don't rise to the challenges that their lives present to them. There's a lot more room for ambiguity and ambivalence. You don't have that pressure to make everything be so plot-driven. I love movies, don't get me wrong. But television is, if you use visual art as a metaphor, a broader canvas. There are more colors to play with.

Littlefield: Give us some examples of excellent feature film scripts.
Ball: *The Apartment* and *To Kill a Mockingbird* are amazing movies. Also, *Nashville* and *Taxi Driver*. These are all movies that had a big impact on me in terms of the power of their storytelling.

Littlefield: Do you have any favorite writing rituals?
Ball: I always listen to music when I write. It's hard for me to write when it's silent. I make specific play lists for specific projects I'm working on. I have a play list of over a thousand songs. One way that I procrastinate is that I will have a scene and it's like, "What needs to be playing in the background?" and then I'll spend an hour on iTunes and $200 later I'll find a song. For *True Blood* I listen to a lot of country music, a lot of alt-country music. Each character and each location in *True Blood* has its own specific feel. I might have a lot of industrial, Nine Inch Nails kind of stuff that is the Fangtasia [a vampire bar in *True Blood*] play list. And a kind of country and folk and honky tonk music that is the Merlotte's [the restaurant-bar where main character Sookie works] play list.

Littlefield: What do you look for when you hire writers for a TV series?
Ball: When I hire writers, I will only read original work. In one case I hired a writer off a short story. It's about whether the writer's real voice meshes with the voice of the show. If somebody has written a great episode for *Breaking Bad* or *Dexter* or *Mad Men*, for example, I don't read those. And if I get a script and there's nothing funny in it, I'm not going to hire that writer. If I get a script and there's nothing meaningful where I have a real glimpse into somebody's personal pain—I'm not going to hire that writer, either. Not for *True Blood*.

Littlefield: Any advice for new writers trying to break into television?
Ball: Write what you care about. Write about things that mean something to you. Write the television show or the movie that you would love to see. Don't think about what the marketplace wants. If those books that give screenwriting formulas help you, that's fine, but don't feel that they're bibles—that those are rules that cannot be broken—because that just makes every movie seem exactly alike. When you do that, you're just closing the door to other possibilities.

• • •

In June 2008, Kinney Littlefield interviewed Alan Ball for an Associated Press story on Ball's new HBO series, *True Blood*. The following material was never published as part of that story and is reprinted here with the permission of the Associated Press 2012.

Ball sat in a director's chair inside the crumbling Louisiana home of series heroine Sookie Stackhouse—actually on the *True Blood* set in Calabasas, California—sipping strong coffee, talking vampires, *True Blood*, and television.

Q: So is *True Blood*'s theme really how we treat outsiders, those who are different?
Ball: Absolutely. It's not really an AIDS metaphor. There's a moment in the third episode where we find out that one of the humans who the vampires are feeding on is infected with—in the show we made it hepatitis D, which is the only blood-born pathogen that vampires are susceptible to. But the show is less about that. It's also about the terrors of intimacy and any kind of misunderstood, hated, feared minority—homosexuals, other cultures. Also, at the same time, it's a metaphor for a group [vampires] that is frighteningly powerful—and ruthless. So it's a metaphor that works both ways. We've actually taken that aspect maybe a little further than it exists in Harris's books.

Q: Why *True Blood* after the huge critical success of *Six Feet Under*?
Ball: After five years of *Six Feet Under*—which was one of the greatest experiences of my life—I felt like, I'm kind of done with peering into the abyss and being stranded in this existential place between life and death, and I want to do something fun. When I first pitched *True Blood* to HBO, I called it "popcorn TV for smart people." It's like an amusement park ride. We end each episode with a cliffhanger. In a way it's got a little bit of an old-fashioned movie serial feel to it.

So *True Blood* is a lot more fun. Charlaine [Harris] has just created this amazing world that's funny and vibrant and scary and also a sort of social treatise, you know what I mean? The books are violent, and that's part of the appeal. It's visceral and predatory and unapologetically sexual. And it's unapologetically romantic in the sense of an old-fashioned romance novel.

Q: What's your personal writing process on the series?
Ball: I have to feel it in my gut. That's what I'm doing with *True Blood*. I actually will bring a cut home and I'll put it in the DVD player and I'll watch it, and fifty-five minutes later I'm like, "Oh shit, I didn't take a single note." I have to go back and watch it. I got so wrapped up in the performances—the actors on the show are so much fun to watch. It's a show I've never really seen before and I get lost in the world. And then I have to go back and start making notes. There are other people who are really good at coming from a very cerebral place. I'm not one of them.

I wanted *True Blood* to be about the characters. I didn't want to give the vampires crazy contact lenses. It's just, "let the actors act it." And I think that's what's really fun about the show is that the cast is so good and they're having so much fun that it's kind of infectious. Again, it's always about the characters.

Q: As a Southerner, originally, how have you crafted the image of the South that we see in the series?

Ball: I am from the South, and I've always hated it when Hollywood goes to the South and everybody is wearing bonnets and it just feels so completely overdone and unrealistic. *True Blood* takes place in a very small town in the South. And I love that aspect of it, that this is a small town where actually people don't spend their time surfing the Web. They don't text message each other. They still live in a less complicated way, because they don't need to do all that stuff, you know what I mean?

And I really wanted to try to keep as much of *True Blood* rooted in nature as possible. I always saw the supernatural as not being something that exists outside of nature but something that is deeper in nature, maybe deeper than we have the perceptional ability to really see.

Q: What effects do you use to create the vampire look on *True Blood*?

Ball: I didn't want *True Blood* to be a heavy visual effects show. We made a point of being very specific with the physiology of the vampires' fangs. They're more like rattlesnakes' fangs. They retract and they stay up against the roof of their [the characters'] mouth until they come out. They sort of pivot down. When we have scenes where the fangs actually extend, we have to do some visual effects to make that work.

I find that the less you see on camera, the more interesting it is. You know when Charlaine Harris describes it in the books, when there are shape-shifters or were-creatures who change, there's a blur and then there's the new creature. I certainly don't want to have that *American Werewolf in London*, long, involved morphing process which was great then, but which we've all seen 150 times. Plus the amount of money it would take to shoot that and add the visual effects to it, I would [need to] shoot three days. This is an expensive TV show, but it's still a TV show. It's not a movie. And I don't want to waste money on stuff that people have already seen.

Q: So what is *True Blood*'s cost per episode?

Ball: You know what, it's embarrassing, but I don't really know what *True Blood*'s cost per episode is . . . I don't. I'm actually—these are not my concerns. And I know that sounds very arrogant, but my brain doesn't work in [those] terms and there are other people at HBO and people who are involved in the show, and that's their job. I prefer it that way. It is expensive, but I don't really know what the budget is.

I know people come to me and they say, "Ah, this is a really expensive episode. Can we move this scene from this location and put it on our location on the stage?" And 95 percent of the time I will say yes because I sort of feel like it's insane to waste money. But I'm very lucky, in that I get to focus on the scripts, and postproduction and everything in the show, and I don't really pay much attention to the money.

Excerpt from Interview with Alan Ball: *True Blood* and Beyond

NANCY HARRINGTON / 2011

From Archive of American Television, emmytvlegends.org, August 25, 2011. Printed by permission.

Q: So let's move on to *True Blood.*
A: Yes.

Q: Can you describe how that series came about?
A: You know I lived in Los Angeles for fifteen years and I still can't figure out how long it's going to take me to get from one place to another. I had an appointment with a dentist in the valley for a root canal. It was some dentist I'd never been to, and I showed up thirty minutes early. So I had a half hour to kill and there was a Barnes and Noble across the street. I was walking up and down the aisles, and I saw this little book. I don't know why I picked it up. It was *Dead Until Dark* by Charlaine Harris, and the tagline was "maybe having a vampire for a boyfriend isn't such a bright idea"—which made me laugh. I bought it, I read it, and I couldn't put it down. I'm from the South; Charlaine's from the South. It had a very authentic Southern feel to it, and there was great mix of drama and comedy and horror and sex and violence and social commentary. She walked this line that was so incredibly entertaining that I couldn't put the book down. There were three more books available at that time, so I got them on Amazon. I read them like crack, and right around book four, I said I think this would make a great TV show. I called my agent, we tried to get in touch with Charlaine, but it was under option to some movie guy. I was like, "Okay, well, you know if the option ever runs out, let me know."

I went and directed a movie. I wrote a play, and then it turned out the rights were available. I spoke to Charlaine, and I said, "This is what I love about your work; this is what I would really fight to maintain. I think it should be a TV show and not a movie. It's too big for a movie, and I would love to do it," and she agreed. I wrote a pilot and two more episodes just to give HBO a sense of what it would be like, and they agreed to produce it. We shot it, and then I didn't hear from them for like three months. It was totally different from the *Six Feet Under* experience, but they finally decided to go ahead with it. They wanted to recast one of the roles, and we did that. And then we did the first season.

Q: Tell us what the premise of the show is?
A: The show takes place in a world where vampires have made their existence known to humans. They've come out of the coffin, so to speak. They're sort of struggling for equal rights, assimilation, but they're also dangerous, exotic creatures. There's a whole group of people called Fangbangers who want to get bitten or have sex with vampires. Vampire blood is a very potent drug, so vampires are being stalked and drained for their blood. This is all seen through the eyes of a very, very small town in Louisiana called Bon Temps. The main character is Sookie Stackhouse who is a waitress and who is telepathic because she has faerie blood. She meets a vampire, and he's the first man she's ever met where she can't hear his thoughts. It allows her to relax and be herself, and they have a love affair. It goes from there.

Q: And what is your role on the show, and has it evolved at all or has it always been the same?
A: It's the same. I created the show, and I didn't. I mean I didn't create the characters or the world. They're source material from the books by Charlaine Harris, but I created the show, and I'm the executive producer, show runner—pretty much exactly what I did on *Six Feet Under*.

Q: Were you always interested in writing the supernatural or is it just because you found these books?
A: I had never read the books. I didn't even know *Twilight* existed. I had never read an Anne Rice book. I never saw an episode of *Buffy* until recently, so it wasn't like, "Oh my God, I want to do a show about vampires!" I think I was looking to do something different. I had peered into the abyss with *Six Feet Under* for five years. I didn't necessarily want to do something that heavy or that existential. I wanted to have fun. And when I read this book, I thought, I can see this show. It's a show for adults. It's fun. It's popcorn. It's got some interesting things to say, but ultimately it's pure entertainment. And I think that's where I want to go right now.

Q: And how does this show differ from the books?
A: Well the books are all narrated by Sookie, so the books are all Sookie's story.

The show is a huge ensemble piece. There are six or seven major characters, and then ten or eleven secondary characters. By now they're all contractually guaranteed every single episode, so we really try to tell the story of all these people in this town at the same time. We're trying to keep it all together, so it's different in that regard. And we've taken some liberties with the story.

Q: What's the reaction from fans of the book when you take liberties, when you stray too far from the books?
A: I know there are people who refer to themselves as book bangers, and they don't like the show. They think the books are better, you know. I don't. I hear from the other writers I work with what people are posting on the boards; I don't go on the boards.

Q: And is Charlaine involved in the series at all?
A: She's not officially involved. I mean she comes out for the premier every year, and she's very sweet and she and I have a really good relationship. She said you have to look at them as two separate things. They are two separate things—the show and the books. She says "I don't tell Alan how to run his show, and he doesn't tell me how to write my books." She's delightful. I think the experience has been mutually beneficial for both of us, so I don't think there's any judgment or animosity one way or the other.

Q: Do you know where she's heading with the books in the future?
A: I don't. I know that she's written ten of them. She plans to write thirteen of them, but I don't know where she's heading.

Q: So you don't have any contractual obligations to stick to her story lines or—?
A: Uh-uh.

Q: Great. And again you're such an auteur. You've created other worlds on your own. Why create her worlds? Why? What drew you to them?
A: It spoke to me. It felt recognizable, not in the sense of vampires and stuff, but the people in the smallness of the town. It's a feedback to my youth; it took me back to when I was kid, when I would go to Blairsville, Georgia, which is this tiny little town in the mountains where my grandfather lived. It took me back to that place that has pretty much disappeared—at least where I grew up in metro Atlanta has become just like every other place in America with a Best Buy and a Wal-Mart. There's a sense (in the books) of a really true regional identity. I really responded to that. I liked the characters, I liked the world. It just felt fun. But obviously, it jived with my own voice in a way because otherwise I don't think I would have responded to it.

Q: What do you think it is about the vampire culture that's such a phenomenon now?

A: I have no idea. I can say I think part of it is the immortality, part of it is they're creatures of the night. They're the ultimate bad boys or bad girls; they're dangerous. I think a lot of women read this type of fiction. They are, at their heart, romance novels. You know there's that idea of it—if only he had the love of a good woman, I could tame the beast in him. I think there is something really powerful about the idea of being taken by a creature that's so outside of the realm of possibility. People can let themselves sort of fantasize about that in a way they wouldn't fantasize about really being taken by somebody stronger than themselves; that's rape. Nobody wants to be raped, but you know rape fantasies are not uncommon. For whatever reason in the last twenty years, vampires have become really handsome and really hot and sexy and there's that brooding, misunderstood, tortured, hot, bad boy who is up late at night, rock star thing.

And they're sexy. Vampires are sex. I mean obviously vampires really sort of became part of pop culture as a metaphor for sex, at a time when sex couldn't really be depicted or acknowledged.

Q: Can you talk a little bit about the writing process on the show?

A: The writing process is different from *Six Feet Under* only in that there is source material. We come in at the beginning of each season. We have a book. We go through the book—this is what we like, this is what we don't like, this is what we'll keep, this is what will veer from, this is what are we going to do with all these other characters who don't have stories in this book. And we very roughly map out where we're going towards the end of the season, and then we start breaking individual stories. Because no matter how much you map out where the season's going to go, it's always going to change. So rather than get really specific in each of these twelve episodes, we'll say somewhere around this episode this person will find out about this and there'll be a big, big showdown in episode twelve. And now let's start doing the end of his role.

Q: There have been varying reports and theories about whether a vampire on a show is a metaphor for gay people? Does that . . . what's your take on that?

A: My take is that the vampire is not a metaphor for gay people. I'm gay myself, I'm not going to say gay people are blood-sucking monsters. I think part of what I enjoyed about the book was the vampire. You know people are striving for vampire rights, and then there are questions of vampire marriage and stuff like that. I think because we live in a time where the gay and lesbian community is struggling for equal rights in a very visible way, it's very easy to say vampires are supposed to be gays and lesbians. If the show was fifty years ago, it'd be African Americans. If it was a hundred years ago, it'd be women. There are times of course where you play the fun of having a spokesperson on TV explaining why vampires should be given equal rights and stuff like that. But it's certainly not a conscious choice, and I don't think it's one that really holds up if you look at it too closely.

Q: And what does the show say about life in the South?
A: I think the show says about life in general that life is much more primal than perhaps we want it to be, that we all have primal urges and desires and that we all have monsters living inside of us. I think because it's in the South it has a sort of swampy, small town, narrow-minded, bigoted aspect to some of the characters. But I don't know if there is that much about life in the South (in the show). I think it says more about the primal nature of being a living, breathing creature of meat and bones. Sort of our fears and desires related to that.

Q: And you're once again touching on the theme of mortality. Do you look at it differently in this show?
A: Yeah, it's different because you have people who don't ever die, so it's very different. It's like a fantasy world. It's not really based in reality. It's like a dream world—a Freudian, Jungian playground. It doesn't really have a lot to do with the real issues of how one makes peace with one's own mortality.

Q: Do you face any kind of censorship on this show?
A: I've never actually had any sort of censorship; I mean there was that one instance where they asked if we could not be quite so graphic with Tara ripping Franklin Mott's neck out with her teeth. But then there was another instance when Maryann was overseeing and sort of creating this orgy out in the woods, and they asked, "Can we see a little more skin, can it be a little hotter? Right now it's not quite hot enough." I think those were the only (instances of) censorship. I mean we're never going to show pornography, I think pornography is about body parts physically—vaginas and penises. We're never going to show that. For me the show is about the characters and their emotions. It's romance. We have a lot of people call it lady porn. Of course we're going to show romance and part of the whole nature of the primal soup of sex and death and supernatural and whatever is sex—making love and those primal urges and desires. So of course we're going to show that, but I don't think we've ever done it in a way that was prurient or specifically body-part focused. None of those actors are going to show those parts of themselves anyway, so we'll never know that. I wouldn't even want to because once you do that, it becomes all about that.

Q: Is there a character that you prefer writing for?

A: I love writing for Lafayette. I love writing for Jason. I love writing for all of them, but I have to say those two are particularly fun. But I do love writing for all the characters.

Q: Let's talk a little bit about the casting process. Do you remember who you cast first and how that process went?

A: Actually the first person we cast was Ryan because I saw him in the movie *Flicka* where he played the dim, hot brother of the heroine, and I was like, "Well that's Jason." I think my only question was, "Are you going to be comfortable depicting that kind of sexuality because this guy is kind of a sex addict. He's like one of those overgrown boys whose only sense of being special comes from how many conquests he has." So he said, "Yeah." So we did. I think we cast a bunch of people all at once. Anna aggressively pursued this, and thank God she did. I think we cast Anna and Sam and then Tara. I don't remember.

Q: Let's do what we did before and go through each character and just talk a little bit about them. Can you describe them and how they've evolved?

A: Okay.

Q: The first is Sookie?

A: Sookie is a person who grew up with the ability to hear other people's thoughts, which turned her into kind of a strange, odd little bird. Then she meets a vampire. She can't hear his thoughts, and she can sort of be herself. Anna and I joked that over the course of the first season, Sookie went from being an innocent virgin to being a murdering whore. Over the course of the show, she has certainly claimed her power. She actually has supernatural power too—her faerie DNA. I think she's got a strong moral center. She wants to do the right thing. She's very emotional. She's had a hard life, but she is not going to be a victim.

Q: And next is Bill?

A: Bill is a guy who was turned against his will, and he lost everything he ever cared about. He's never been fully comfortable embracing his vampire nature 100 percent. He wants to retain his humanity, and when he met Sookie, he felt like he had been given a second chance at happiness and life. Unfortunately he met her because he'd been sent to seduce her for the Queen of Louisiana, and she found that out. Things went awry, but he still loves her and he still wants to be a good guy.

Q: What about Eric?

A: Eric doesn't really want to be a good guy, Eric's probably the most—Eric and Pam are probably the most—comfortable in their vampire skin. Eric was a warrior. Eric was a cocky young prince whose family was murdered and then he went off to avenge it. Then he was dying and was made vampire. I think Eric definitely has got a heart, but I think he is not even remotely sentimental. It's not until he meets Sookie that he feels like humans are really anything to be taken in any other way than food or sex. But something about her touches something about him, and then of course in the most recent season, he's kind of a different version of himself. He's taken through witchcraft back to a sort of younger, more innocent, more vulnerable side of himself, which of course is what Sookie falls in love with, but that's not the real Eric.

Q: How about Sam?
A: Sam . . . you know all these characters seem to be orphans in one way or another. Sam is a guy who was adopted as a baby, and when he shape shifted at age fifteen, his parents abandoned him. They moved away, so he was on his own at a very early age. Sam has a hard time trusting people, but he's a good guy. He's capable of some bad shit. He's killed. He's now just trying to make a life for himself and do the right thing.

Q: Do have any favorite episode of *True Blood*?
A: Of *True Blood*?

Q: Yeah.
A: Yeah, I love the episode where we see Bill being made. We go back to the Civil War, and we see him become a vampire. I loved the episode where Mary-ann throws a big party for Tara and it turns into a Dionysian, Bacchanalian party of excess. I love that one. I love all the flashbacks of Eric as a Viking. Let's see . . . this year I love the episode where—it hasn't aired yet—where they're all trapped inside Moon Goddess and the vampires are outside with weapons. I think it's a really, really strong, really, really fun episode. I like all the episodes, but those are the ones that jump to mind immediately. I love the episode where Tommy skin walks as Sam.

Q: And you also wrote and produced six mini episodes, that sort of teased season three. So how did those come about and why do you think they were important to do?
A: HBO asked if we would be open to the idea of doing mini-sodes, and I said yeah. Then they took a crack at them, and I looked at what they gave us, and I said, "I think I should write these because I know the show, and I'll know what to do." So I wrote them. In terms of producing, I really wasn't on the stage when they were shot because they were all being shot by directors that

are pretty much part of our family now. I knew that everything would be okay. But yeah I was involved in the editing.

Q: And how important of a role do you think the Internet plays in the series?
A: I don't know. I think the Internet was very important in the launch of the series. I know that Jessica has a blog that my assistant Gianna writes and does a wonderful job with, that people go to. In terms of fans of the show and posting on the boards and that kind of stuff, I don't pay any attention to that. I know that we have created fake websites to sort of extend the reality of the show. There's a Fellowship of the Sun website. There's an American Vampire League website. This year there's a www.vamps-kill.com website. But I think that's all just like added stuff. I think the show could exist without the Internet. I mean we also have the comic books which are part of the cannon.

Q: You just got picked up for a fifth season?
A: Yes.
Q: Congratulations.
A: Thank you.
Q: Can you tease anything for us?
A: Can I tease anything? We are definitely going to get under the surface of the vampire hierarchy. They're going to get into the Authority and see what that is and what it means. And that's some fun that we'll be doing in season five.

Q: Now we're just going to wrap up.
A: Okay.

Q: What other current projects do you have going on?
A: My company is overseeing a show called *Banshee*, which is going to go to Cinemax, that was written by Jonathan Tropper and David Schickler. It's a real sort of pulpy, fun, noir series set in Pennsylvania in Amish country, and they've written three episodes. It's a really good show. I think we're going to start shooting that in the spring of 2012, and I'm excited about that. My company has a lot of other shows in development at HBO, but nothing that's going up at the point for me to talk about. We are producing a TV movie based on the book *The Immortal Life of Henrietta Lacks* with Oprah's company, which I'm excited about. I've got some movies I'm trying to put together, but it's so hard. It's so hard to get a movie done right now if it's not a comic-book movie or a gross-out comedy. But I'm not going to stop trying.

Q: What do you think the key to creating a successful TV show is?
A: I don't think there's any one key, I think there's a lot of elements that have to come together. But if I had to pick one, I'd have to say characters—characters

NANCY HARRINGTON / 2011   **113**

that people want to spend time with, characters that people are going to invest in, characters that people are going to care about what happens to them. That's the result of both writing and casting, and hopefully those two can meld in a way that people want to tune in each week to see what happens to these people. I think no matter how interesting the story is, if we don't care about the people, they're not going to tune in. I always say that if *True Blood* was a presidential campaign we would have a sign in the writers' room that said: "It's the emotions stupid." Because you can come up with as many outlandish, vampire, werewolf, pyrotechnics, but unless you care about these people, then it's just going to be meaningless. So I would say you got to have people that you care about in the show.

Q: And do you have advice for someone starting out as a television writer/producer?

A: My advice for somebody starting out in TV is to write a show that you would watch. Write the show that you would want to see, that, at the very least, you'll have a nice writing sample. I mean my advice may be the wrong advice for somebody, but I know that every time I've tried to sort of look at the marketplace and say I think there's an audience for this or think that this is something that could sell, I have failed miserably. I have been successful when I wrote things I really cared about, stories that I felt like I would watch, I would get invested in. My second thing would be, don't wait for permission. Don't wait for somebody to say you can do it. Get a camera. Get a flip camera, get a D7 camera, start shooting your own stuff. Make your own stuff. You don't have to wait for people to give you permission. What you want to do is to develop your voice, and the best way to do that is to do it on your own. That would be my advice.

Q: And if you had to pick one thing what would be the highlight of your career so far?

A: The highlight of my career? Phew, you know I don't know. I don't know what it would be, I don't think in those terms. I think just the fact that I get to do what I do feels like the biggest gift that I could ever hope for. The fact that I, through some combination of hard work and perseverance and luck, have stumbled into this position where I can really make stuff that I would watch and that I have a really good time doing and working with such amazing people. I mean that's the high point. And I've been lucky enough for that to kind of be an ongoing thing, and I hope it continues.

Q: Where do you see yourself in ten years?

A: Ten years? I'll be sixty-four; I won't be running a TV show, I'll tell you that. I don't know. I would like to be able to continue work in different mediums, television, film, theater, but I would like to have a less stressful existence. [laughs] But I don't know. I don't know where I'll be in ten years. I don't know.

Q: Well, we hope you'll be making great TV shows.
A: Well, thank you. [laughs] Thank you.

Alan Ball in Conversation with Alan Brough

ALAN BROUGH / 2011

Event hosted by the Wheeler Centre (cosponsored by the Sydney Opera House), September 10, 2011. Printed by permission.

Q: Welcome, Alan.
A: Thank you. It's great to be here.

Q: Before we start, you are from Georgia originally. I believe that while you were still living in Georgia, someone opened a shop there where you could just go in and shoot things.
A: Yeah. When I was in high school, I heard about this place where if you were mad at a TV you could take it to this business and you could shoot it. I remember thinking, why can't you just shoot it in your own backyard? Wow, that is pretty indicative of the Georgia mentality. "Oh, I can shoot it myself, but why when I can pay someone to shoot a television."

Q: What are your fondest memories of the Ball household when you were growing up?
A: (laughs) When I was born in 1957, I was growing up in a small town that was not yet part of the metropolitan Atlanta sprawl. So we lived in this new subdivision right at the edge of the woods, and as kids we would spend a lot of time in the woods. Actually I remember that quite fondly and that sort of connection to nature. Probably one of the most fond memories was leaving. It's a beautiful area of the country, and there is a tremendous literary tradition. But it was not a place I could stay.

Q: Were you always eager to get out?
A: No, I very much wanted to belong. I guess at some point really early on I realized I was different, and I desperately wanted to be normal. But alas, it was not meant to be.

Q: In that vein, who was a first person who you met that made you think—Oh my God, I've never met anyone like you—and through that, sort of changed you?

A: I remember going to see movies. The first movie I went to see was a mov-ie called *My Six Loves*, and it was about an American movie star, played by Debbie Reynolds, who through some wacky turn of events became the fos-ter-mother for six adorable Ozark children. It was an early sixties movie. Of course, over the course of the movie, she realized that "I don't want to be a successful actress with a career. What I really want to be is a wife and mother." But I remember the big screen and sort of the magnificence of it all. I remem-ber that. I don't remember meeting that many people, honestly, in Marietta, Georgia. Somehow, it was just through movies and TV that I realized I had to get out of there. I remember going to a play—the first time I saw a play. I saw *Cat on a Hot Tin Roof* at the Alliance Theatre in Atlanta, Georgia. This was before the Internet and before computers and everything. I'm really dating myself. I think there was just really something in me that knew that this is not where I'm supposed to be.

Q: Well, you ended up getting a theatre arts degree, and—
A: I actually did not get the degree.
Q: Oh, you didn't get the degree?
A: I dropped out. I'm a college dropout. Yes. Years later after I achieved a cer-tain level of success, my university called and said, "We'd like to give you an honorary Ph.D." I said, "Thank you, but I actually am kind of proud of the fact that I did it on my own. So, no thanks."

Q: Were they horrified that you turned them down?
A: I don't know. I don't know if they were horrified or not. It wasn't anyone I had ever known from the college. They just said: "Well . . . okay . . . thank you."

Q: So you dropped out, but you ended up as a playwright.
A: Yes. When I was in college, I had a double major in acting and playwriting, which was kind of odd because there was no playwriting instructor or classes. I don't know. What they let us do is they let us write shows and produce them in the basement. This was in the mid-seventies right when *Saturday Night Live* first hit the airwaves. We stared doing sketch comedy shows in the base-ment. That's really how I got my start—doing sketch comedy. As a writer, it's a great way to start because even if it's just a two-page sketch, it still has to have a beginning, middle, and end. I kind of went from there to one-act to full-length plays. But I always had a company of like-minded people, and we were working in basements and on Thursday nights at midnight. There were

usually more people on stage than there were in the audience. But it was a total labor of love, and I spent many, many years doing it where it wasn't a vocation. It wasn't a job. It was for the sheer love of it. And I'm really grateful for that because it cemented a kind of way of approaching the work that I still hope I've retained a bit.

Q: How did you move from writing two-page sketches in basements at midnight to writing on sitcoms like *Grace Under Fire* and *Cybill*, which you were even a co-executive producer on?
A: Yes.

Q: How did you get there?
A: Well, I moved to New York in 1986, and a lot of people I had gone to college with were living in New York. And we started a little theater company. We were doing one acts. Then I wrote a full-length play called *Five Women Wearing the Same Dress* about bridesmaids in Knoxville, Tennessee, at a big stupid wedding and they all hated the bride. So they hung out in the bride's sister's bedroom during the reception. It was southern women and wacky comedy, and somebody from Carsey-Warner television either read it or saw it, and I got an offer to write for *Grace Under Fire*, which was a sitcom that I had never heard of. I just figured, "Well how many times is this going to happen?" By that time, all the people in the theater company, you know, their day-jobs had turned into careers. They had gotten married and started having children. So it was really just a hobby for everybody else. And I kind of realized, well that's all it's ever going to be, that's all this company is every going to be. So I'll take this job. I moved out to LA on a Friday, and I started working on a Monday. My first job was *Grace Under Fire*, which was the perfect first job because nothing will ever be that bad. It was a real crash course in writing. It's not like in the theater where people have a certain amount of respect for the script or the text, as we call it. It was completely different. I spent a year on that show and three years on *Cybill*, and if I had turned those in, I would have hit the trifecta.

I wouldn't trade those years for anything, but at the time, it was not a pleasant experience. I became sort of like a factory worker. I learned a lot of rules about what you did, what the network wanted, and what the star wanted. By the time I got to *Cybill*, we would start every episode with the question: "Okay, what's the moment of shit in this episode?" Which was the moment when Cybill's daughter would cry and say, "Mom, I guess the reason I was mad at you is because when you were my age you really knew what you were doing and you had everything figured out. I guess I'm just jealous because I'll never be as great as you." And it was really horrifying. I also learned that all the notes from the network came back and they were basically—make everybody nicer and articulate the subtext. That's the moment of shit.

I had done two years on *Cybill*, and I decided to take a year off and write something I care about. Because if I don't, I'm going to hate myself. I can't do this. They said, "What if we gave you more money than you ever dreamed possible?" And I said, "Okay. I'll do one more year, and I'll put it in the bank. Then, I'll take the year off." I actually couldn't wait because I felt like such a whore . . . because I was. I would come home from writing moments of shit, and I would just pour myself into this really angry screenplay, which was *American Beauty*. It's no coincidence that it is the story of a man who is a writer—granted a technical writer at a trade magazine—who has lost his passion for living and gets it back in a really inappropriate way. In the process, I sort of reclaimed my own passionate connection to my work. I was very blessed that all the stars aligned, that all the right people came together, and that it became what it became.

Q: When *American Beauty* came out, how did you expect it was going to go? And when did you get an inkling as to how it was actually going?
A: When I was on the set every day when we were shooting, I could tell that the actors were really good, and Sam was really good, and it was really coming together in a way that I thought was really true to the script, and I'm going to be proud to be part of this. Nobody ever thought it would become this sort of phenomenon that it did. We all thought it would be a little art house movie that some people would like, but it would come and go and live on DVD. Then there was some writer who came to see a screening of it, and he wrote this piece for the *New York Times*. He sort of got all hyperbolic about it, and I sort of went, "Okay." Then it came out, and the reviews started coming out and they were saying the most amazing things, which as a writer you really want to believe. And it did really well at the box office. Then DreamWorks started calling me and saying, "We want you to go to this film festival and go talk to this radio show." It was very surreal.

At the same time, I had developed this situation comedy for one of the broadcast networks because I had signed a TV development deal a week before I sold the script to *American Beauty*. So I created this show about three guys living in a brownstone in Brooklyn with a dog named Mom, who would bark and there would be subtitles. And that was *not* as well received. There was literally an issue in *People* magazine that was the best and worst of 1999 where literally on the page where it said "The Top Ten Movies" and it listed *American Beauty* you would turn the page and it said "The Ten Worst Television Shows." There was a blurb that said, "This is first television show that is actually physically painful to watch." So it was a great lesson in balance.

Q: Was it physically painful to make?
A: At the time, no. I went through this whole cognitive dissonance. When I

first pitched it, it was very much in the vein of that great British sitcom *The Young Ones*. And by the time it reached the airwaves (at that time I have to take every note the network gives me, that's what you do), it was three really handsome guys in designer clothes trading insults. And there was a moment of shit in every episode. By the time it reached the air, I sort of developed this cognitive dissonance where I was massively invested in a show I actually did not like myself. Because I knew that 150 people were employed and I was trying to keep it on the air. It got cancelled. I was heartbroken at the time, but thank God it did because then I got to do *Six Feet Under*.

Q: I want to talk about *Six Feet Under*, but I want to ask you something first. In 2000, after you won the Oscar for Best Original Screenplay, how differently were you and your work judged?
A: I think people all of a sudden felt like I knew what I was talking about. I was the same guy and the same writer prior to that. But when I was developing the sitcom for ABC, every time I would pitch something, they said, "Yes, but what if you did it differently." And after the Oscar and more importantly after the profitability of *American Beauty*, which was a very cheap little movie that made a lot of money for a lot of people—not me so much. . . . No, I'm not bitter—then I would say something and everyone would say, "Wow . . . wow."

Q: Did that change the way you judged yourself?
A: No. The fact that I'm sort of an insider is hilarious to me because my whole psyche, my whole sense of identity is based very much on being an outsider, so prior to the Oscars, I was the guy who would watch the Oscars on TV and throw a ball of socks at the screen and yell at it and drink every time somebody did something totally embarrassing. And then I was sitting there in the audience, and people were doing these massively embarrassing things, and I was like "Oh, my God." I had a flask in my pocket. I was pretty much out of my body the whole time. It seemed like, "What are you doing here? This is for someone else. . . . No, no." I hope I answered your question.

Q: You did. Well, I'm just wondering if you were out of body to begin with, how out of body were you when they read your name out as the winner?
A: It is the most surreal thing ever. You get up. You walk down, and then you get on stage and look out and the first thing you see is a big TV monitor at the back of the auditorium that starts going: *20 . . . 19 . . . 18 . . .* "What is that? Why are those numbers . . . ? Oh, I have to talk really fast." Your voice is shaking. That was before I discovered beta blockers. It was very surreal.

Q: After you win an Oscar, all of a sudden everyone is calling you, offering you work. Some of it good, some of it not so good, and I just wondered what was the most inappropriate thing that you were being offered after you won the Oscar?

A: Pretty much everything that I was offered was male, mid-life stories, but I had done that. I remember being asked to meet on a story about drag queens in prison who put on some sort of musical. One of them fell in love with one of the prison wardens. I remember thinking, Really? You want to make that movie? You want me to write it? I actually did a couple of drafts on some movies, but that's the one that sticks out in my mind.

Q: In an interview I read, I think it was in *New York Magazine*, you said, "My mantra is: 'This is just a TV show. It's not worth going crazy, getting sick over, or becoming a drug addict for.'" I wonder how hard was it to stay sane, well, and unaddicted when you were working on *Six Feet Under*, given thematically and story-wise what was being dealt with on that show week in and week out?

A: It wasn't difficult at all. I went through my insane, bad-behavior period those years I was working on the sitcoms. I had moved from New York to LA where I didn't have that many friends, and LA can be a really existentially lonely city. But *Six Feet Under* I really loved, and I was working with great people, and even though the subject matter itself could be viewed as depressing, it was such a great experience. I think I probably struggled a bit with workaholism, but it was fun going to work every day because I worked with great writers and I worked with a tremendous class. In a lot of ways for me, it was like film school. I was learning so much that oddly enough it wasn't depressing. Once I went back into TV and did *True Blood*, which is so ridiculous and silly and fun, I realized, "This is a lot more fun than *Six Feet Under*." I know that it was a little depressing for some of the actors, but it wasn't for me. Again, it's just a TV show. It's not real life.

Q: Before, you mentioned that when you worked on *Cybill* you got notes back from the network saying "make everyone nicer." Is it true that when you wrote the pilot from *Six Feet Under* you got a note from HBO asking you to make it weirder?

A: The actual words were: "We really like it. The whole thing feels just a little safe. Could you just go in there and make the whole thing a little more fucked up?" I was like, "Yeah. Seriously? You want me to do that?" Actually the first couple of seasons of *Six Feet Under*, I realized I had to unlearn the lessons I had learned on the sitcoms because I know what note we're going to get, so let's just have Zoey say: "Oh, I know, I guess I was just jealous about how together you were." We don't have to state the subtext, and people don't have to be nice to each other all the time. Actually, it can be kind of like real life. "Yeah, I would love to do that." That's in a nutshell why it's such a joy to work at someplace like HBO because they really do want something that has a specific voice. On HBO, the show itself is the product; whereas on the broadcast networks—no matter how great the material is, no matter how great a show can be (and there are a lot of great shows on broadcast networks)—the purpose for them is to be a delivery system for the advertising. They want the broadest possible audience, and they also want the programming to exist in this world where everything is vaguely pleasant and explained, and everything works out because that's the same message that the advertisers are telling you. A really great life is possible, and there is a world that is very safe and not threatening and not crazy as long as you buy these products.

Q: When you work on a show like *Six Feet Under* or *True Blood* during pre-production for a season, plot-wise, story-line wise, do you know exactly what is going to happen for the entire season? Or are you often surprised by where characters and storylines take you and the other writers?

A: It's different because for *Six Feet Under* we were just making it up, and *True Blood* is based on source material. But at the beginning of the season, we go in a room and we have twelve columns for each episode and we have different colored pens for each major character. We go through, and we sort of say, "This is going to happen and this is going to happen." You give yourself a sort of broad idea of where you are going to end up, but by the time you hit episode six or seven, you start to rewrite that back end of the season. So I guess the answer is yes and no. You do sort of give yourself a rough destination, but once you get into the actual meat and potatoes of each particular episode, things are going to change. Part of my job is to recognize what the show wants to be and where it wants to go and get out of its way.

Q: Now the source material for *True Blood* is the *Southern Vampire Mysteries*. How did you actually come into contact with it?

A: Total fluke. I've lived in LA for about sixteen years now, and I still can't figure out how long it takes to get from point A to point B because LA is so big and crazy. I had an appointment with an endodontist, a root canal specialist, in Van Nuys, and usually I'm late. But for whatever reason on this day, I was a half hour early, so I went to a Barnes and Noble across the street, wandering up and down the aisles. I don't know what made me pick up this book. If I believed in fate, I would say it was fate, but I don't. So I picked up *Dead Until Dark*, which is the first book in the series, and the tag line read: *Maybe having a vampire for a boyfriend isn't such a good idea.* It kind of made me chuckle. I took it home and started reading it, and I couldn't put it down. It was such a great mix of comedy and horror and romance and sex and violence and social commentary and farce. It was all very authentically Southern because Charlaine is from Arkansas, and I recognized that being a Southerner myself. By the time I got into book four (there were only four available at that time so that was six years ago), I thought I would watch this if it was a TV show. There are such great characters, and it has such a unique tone, I think I would like to pursue the rights to this. They were not available at the time, but a couple of years went by and they became available. And here we are.

Q: What is the process? How do you use the books? Is it one per season? And how do you take that book and make it into a show?
A: Up until this point, it has been one per season. I think probably for season five we're going to start to combine books. The biggest challenge and the most liberating for myself and the other writers is that the books are all narrated by Sookie, so they are basically Sookie's story. All of the other characters don't really exist unless they are in the room with Sookie, or she is thinking about them. So we just sort of take the Sookie stories—though sometimes we change them and make slight adjustments and variations. It is coming up with the stories for the other characters that is the real impetus for coming up with new stories. Then there are things like, for example, in the books Lafayette dies at the beginning of the second book. But I knew when I was shooting the pilot when Nelsan Ellis came on and started improvising, he was channeling from planet Lafayette, and I was like, "I'm not going to kill this character. This guy is too good. It's too great." Then in the first book as well, it's Eric who stakes Longshadow instead of Bill. Then you hear that Eric had to go appear before some council. It made more sense to us for it to be Bill because he is protecting Sookie, and I knew then, having read all the books, that he had been sent by the Queen of Louisiana (I can't believe the plot of this story; it's so hilarious.). We were thinking that the worst punishment for him—being the reluctant vampire he is; he is still mourning and grieving his lost humanity—would be to make him make a vampire. So we made up that character. It is a very organic process. It's me and five other writers. We just sort of go where organically we feel is the best place to go.

Q: There is a lot of man eye-candy in *True Blood.* Is that just for your own personal pleasure or are you attempting to redress the fact that women have been objectified for so long that men should be objectified too?
A: Yes. (pause) Truthfully, at heart the books are romance novels or, as I like to term them, lady porn. And I've discovered that there is a whole subgenre of supernatural romance where there is a human heroine and lots of hot werewolves, shape shifters, angels, fairies, demons, vampires, whatever. It certainly felt to me like the real heart of what *True Blood* is about is just the primal muck that's our psyches, our souls grow out of. And sex is certainly a big part of that. For whatever reason, if you had to say who is the target audience (although I think the show can be enjoyed by anybody), the target audience is women. Believe me, if the actresses were as comfortable taking off their clothes as the

actors are, I would have naked women as much as the guys, but I basically let the actor's comfort level dictate what's going to happen.

Q: And that's interesting because shooting some of the sex scenes—intense to say the least. How difficult is it to take them seriously when you're shooting them? Because I imagine up close, it doesn't look anywhere near as glamorous as it does on screen.

A: Oh, no, no. It's not. I remember when I shot the pilot. I had written the scene, and the character Jason Stackhouse is basically a sexually compulsive guy—who because he's kind of a wounded little boy at heart, his sexual exploits are his main source of self-esteem. So, I had written, *Jason is going down on this woman, and they're both totally naked.* Then I was directing it. The actors show up in bathrobes, and they just take off their clothes. And she's got a little modesty patch, and he's got a little pouch that we call the "sock of destiny." And I was like, "Well, okay folks, just act normal—just talk to them. They are both completely naked, and this isn't awkward at all." But now I don't really do any directing. Basically, the script will say: *And Bill and Sookie make love. Cut.* Then it's up to the writer of that episode, and the director, and the actors. Then I look at the dailies, and I'm like, "Whoa! Wow! I didn't expect that. Okay!" There was actually a point this year where Joe Manganiello, who plays Alcide, comes in and gets undressed and gets in bed with his crazy werewolf girlfriend, and I just said, "He strips down to his boxers." Joe was like, "No, he sleeps naked." And I'm thinking this is going to look so gratuitous, but he has worked really hard on that body and wants to show it off. Who am I to—

Q: Exactly. It would be cruel not to let him. Now, there's vampires, obviously, and werewolves and witches and there's been a few other supernatural creatures. Are there any particularly that you want to have involved? You're going back to shoot another season soon. Trolls, zombies, Sasquatch?

A: [Laughs] I don't necessarily want to go to zombies because there is another show that's all about zombies. And zombies don't really feel like our show. It feels like a different thing. But we had the maenads season two, and we've actually done our research and discovered some other less well-known supernatural creatures that we're going to bring into season five that will be kind of fun. But I'm not going to give any of that away.

Q: Now about the vampires. You say it's easy to look at vampires as a metaphor for any feared group or misunderstood people, and you ciphered gays, political administrations, and people of color. Is that fluidity great as a writer because no matter what social, political, or emotional stuff you want to deal with, the metaphor of the vampire can embody that?

A: Yeah. You know that's all in the books—vampires struggling for assimilation and Congress debating vampire rights and stuff like that, which I thought was hilarious. Because it relates to what is going on in America right now, it's very easy to look at gays and lesbians' struggle for equal rights and marriage rights and say, "That's what the vampires are a metaphor for," but I think that's too simplistic because, on the one hand, they are a misunderstood and feared subculture, but on the other hand, they're dead and they're bloodthirsty monsters. So, as a gay man myself, I'm not going to say, "So, gays and lesbians are bloodthirsty monsters and dead." We actually won an award from the Gay and Lesbian Alliance Against Defamation for being the most positive portrayal of gays on TV, which I thought, *Really?* It was up on the East Coast (we were working, so I wasn't able to go), but Denis O'Hare, who plays Russell Edgington, the King of Louisiana, went. He said, "Is there anything I should say?" And I said, "Yeah, you should thank them for their recognition of our very positive portrayal of gays and lesbians as drug dealing-prostitutes and monsters." And that's exactly what he did.

Q: Now, fans of *True Blood* are incredibly passionate about it. Because of social networks and the Internet, they can get their incredibly passionate views out into the world very loudly.
A: Yes.
Q: And I wonder whether you and the other writers have to be careful not to let those views influence what you're with doing with the show.
A: I don't go on the boards. I don't read those things. First of all, I work so hard that the last thing I want to do when I get home is go online and say, "Oh, what did any random person with a computer think about this week's episode?" I've learned that no matter what you do, there's going to be somebody who *really* hates it and *really* hates you. And there are going to be people who *really* love it and *really* think that everything you do is spectacular and magnificent. Both of those are completely unhelpful because, ultimately, it's about the work. I just feel like it's too confusing if I read something that is really negative. I read something online after I directed this movie called *Towelhead*. After it came out, this guy writes that if anyone sees me that they should punch me in the face. And I was like, "Okay, I'm never going back to this website." You know, it hurt. It hurt my feelings because I'm a writer. I'm not a really thinned-skinned, overly-sensitive freak. Then you read other things where you're like— "Oh, my god, some of the [wonderful] things they've said about *American Beauty*"—and you're tempted to believe it. That's equally destructive. I try really hard to just to do the best work I can do and stay out of the results because, ultimately, it's not about the results; it's about the work. And that's the reward. Whether or not something becomes a hit or it wins awards or people on the Internet like it or they hate it, that stuff is just weather. Sometimes it's good, sometimes it's bad. But it always passes.

Q: I've always been impressed by the depth and truthfulness of the young women you create like Claire in *Six Feet Under*, Angela in *American Beauty*, and Sookie in *True Blood*. Where does your understanding of those young women come from?

A: You know they asked this question in Sydney, and I have to admit I've got a big girl living inside me. A lot of my friends when I was growing up were girls. I had a sister who was eight years older than me, who was probably one of the most influential people in my life. I don't really look at female characters as female characters any more than I look at gay characters as gay characters or straight characters as straight characters. I just feel like characters are characters. I'm a writer within myself and I work with other writers, and I definitely have some really, really good, strong, passionate women on staff, who will stand up and fight for Sookie or Claire because the guys on staff—well, we're guys, not women. We don't have that experience. We're not seeing things as perhaps we should.

Q: Those young women could so easily fall victim to the situations that they find themselves in but refuse to. And I suppose I'm particularly thinking of Jasira in *Towelhead*. Is the refusal to be a victim something close to your heart and personal experience?

A: Yeah. I've seen people cling to victimhood, and it's not pretty. It doesn't help. In regards to *Towelhead*, that's part of the book. And that's the novel *Towelhead* by Alicia Erian, which I read and I really love because here is this story that is usually told as a 100 percent story of victimization. Young women are molested or involved in inappropriate sexual relationships with older men. That's a very common experience. And for it to always be told as a tale of victimization—I didn't realize until I read *Towelhead* how refreshing it was to see this story told in a way where she refused to be a victim. She went through this horrible experience, and Aaron Eckhart's character did a really bad thing, but she wasn't destroyed by it. She wasn't doomed to a life of not being able to enjoy her sexuality because she had been victimized. There was something so great about and refreshing about that take on it that that's why I responded to it and why I wanted to make that movie. I mean it's such a horrible thing. It is a horrible thing. But it's so common. And I hate how the paradigm that we have created to be able to deal with it is one of such victimization because that's really simplistic.

Q: (to the audience) It's a perfect time to now ask for questions from the floor. It's all yours . . .

Q: I just want to ask you: How do you approach your writing, aside from when you're actually working for a show with other writers? Like do you set time in the morning or a particular time of the day when you have a project or whatever?

A: I don't. I'm terribly undisciplined in that regard. I'm very nocturnal. I write late at night. I also listen to music when I write. A lot of times I will. One of my ways to procrastinate is like: "What song would be on the radio in this scene?" I'll just go to iTunes. Two hundred dollars later and two hundred songs that 90 percent of which I'm going delete once I really listen to them. But I do find music is helpful in creating a mood. I kind of just write my own inspiration. My schedule is so weird because on this day—because it's a vampire show and it shoots at night a lot—I'm on the set until 3:00 AM, so I'm not going to get up at 6:00 to write. That's just a longwinded way of saying I'm very undisciplined and I just rely on inspiration. That's a bad answer because I should be telling you how you have to be disciplined.

Q: You said in an interview once that writing for TV makes you technically part of the problem. Are there any steps you take to keep your work from being ideologically corrupted or mainstreamed?

A: Honestly, I feel very fortunate in that I get to work on HBO because I don't ever feel like I've ever gotten a bad note. When I wrote an episode of *Grace Under Fire* about a chiropractor who helps Grace overcome something, they said, "Oh, we can't do that. We have a lot of pharmaceutical and medical people who are advertisers, so can you change the story?" But I don't really have any of that. What I also try to do is I try to mix it up and write in different mediums. You know I wrote a play four years ago. First play in eleven years and that was nice because it reminded me of what it's like to write to just sort of lose yourself in language and not have to tell everything so visually. I've written a bunch of screenplays that will never ever get produced because there uncommercial, but I feel like it's good for me as a writer to try—instead of writing a story with twenty characters that takes place over five years just—to mix it up and sort of not get in the habit of "Oh, this is the thing I do. I'm just going to do it over and over again."

Q: Out of all the people you've worked with over the years (crew members, cast members), who is your favorite person to work with?

A: That is tough because there are a lot of people I've really loved working with. It was not Cybill Shepherd. I really love working with Frances Conroy. She is so dear and such a great actress. I remember doing the scene in the pilot of *Six Feet Under* where she falls apart at the grave of her husband. Snot is coming out of her nose, and she is shaking. I kept thinking, Oh, my God, this is amazing, this is amazing. Then I said, "Cut. Franny that was so wonderful, but I want to get a slightly different coverage. Do you mind if we do it again?" She's like, "Oh yeah, sure." I just saw this woman's soul fall apart. She's such an amazing actress that she does that and then she says, "Okay, what do you want me to do next?" Sometimes, I actually felt if I gave Franny a script that says "Ruth eats a puppy," that she would say, "Well, I've never really eaten a puppy . . . but I'll do it." There is something about that willingness just to dive into a character and go wherever they go and not have any of that "I would never do that. That's not what I would do in that situation." She is just such a pure actress, and such a dear, dear, sweet, wonderful human being. It's a joy to work with somebody like that.

Q: With *American Beauty*, a lot of people connected with it because you probably captured their lives on screen and the culture of Los Angeles. Has that culture at all changed since you have lived there? Have you seen that capitalistic dream change?

A: I feel like America is headed straight to hell in a hand basket. I feel like it is in the process of becoming a totally fascist, horrible place. I'm looking at real estate here. I'm going to need to get out of America at some point in the next few years because it has gotten so bad. Maybe something will happen to reverse that. I hope so. But things are really sad there. Also, Hollywood has gotten worse. *American Beauty* would not be made today. That's depressing too. I'm actually going to call and not go back to America.

Q: You mentioned earlier tonight that you were on the set every day of *American Beauty*'s shooting and that was discussed quite heavily through the social network last year. Can you discuss how relevant that was and how much you did? Or whether they would have stuck to the script verbatim?

A: When I sold the script, I said, "I want to be a part of this. I want to be on set." And they said, "Yes, absolutely." I don't fool myself for a minute that if Sam and I had not been on the same page and wanted to tell the same story and if I had been one of those pushy writers who tried to direct it myself, that they would've said, "Okay, bye-bye." I basically just sat and watched. Occasionally, I was there as a resource. Occasionally, when an actor would be improvising or paraphrasing a line that I felt it was really important that it be the way it was written, I would speak up. That only happened once or twice. I was really like the guest on the set. Because it was my first movie, because it was my first experience with single camera because I had only done sitcoms, I was just sort of really polite. I just sat and watched and told everybody how great they were.

Q: I have a question about characters. What do you think it is about your characters that make them so interesting to an audience—particularly since *Towelhead* and *True Blood* are not your generated characters? In your created characters, do you think dark humor has anything to do with how popular they are with audiences?

A: I'm drawn to characters—whether or not I create them or whether I recognize them in some other source material that somebody has written—who are really struggling on a journey to be authentically who they are in a world that is increasingly inauthentic. I'm interested in people who make mistakes but who are deeply human. I have to feel a lot of affection for the characters. Maybe that is something that people can recognize. I do go to see a lot of movies, and there are heroes and villains. And I'm not really interested in that. I certainly strive to be a well-adjusted person who can confront most of the obstacles that come my way in a sort of effective and functional way. I want that kind of person in my life, but as characters, I find them really boring. I like people who are messing up, who are getting it wrong, but who are trying to figure it out and trying to have meaningful lives. Maybe that is something everybody can relate to.

Q: Could you share some of your insights into the writing process and any tips that you might have—other than listening to music—for aspiring writers?
A: I think every writer, every artist of any kind, has to go on a journey to discover what your process is. I don't think there is any one process or any one way of approaching work that is better than any other. I would say, "Really try to listen to your inner voice in figuring out what the best way you can work is." Just speaking from my own experience, I've been most successful when I've worked on things that I myself would enjoy as an audience member, stories that I myself would enjoy watching, that I would get emotionally involved in. There have been many times when I've said, "Well, I think this is something that will sell right now, or I think this is what the network is looking for. This is what the studios are looking for." I'm very lucky that I've failed miserably every time I've done that. I feel like you have to maintain some emotional connection with your work. Otherwise, you're just purely a craftsperson. There is nothing wrong with that, but I think it's the emotional connection that gives it something extra that audiences respond to. That's my advice: just listen to your heart. That sounds like a real moment of shit. But it's not. If we hugged, it would be a moment of shit.

Q: Some comments have been made about how much Michele Bachmann looks like one of the vampires in *True Blood*. I'd like to hear you comment on that. But on a more serious note, in Australia we watch a lot of television on box sets. Does that happen in America and does that impact your writing style?
A: It actually does. I think of the show that way. I feel like each episode is a chapter. I myself now watch box sets of TV, and I'll watch an episode and think I'll just watch one more. That was part of the joy for me in reading Charlaine's books. I was still working on *Six Feet Under* at the time, and I would have a 6:00 AM call, and I would say to myself, "I'm just going to read

one chapter before I go to bed." Then I would get to the end of the chapter, and it would say, "And Gran's dead on the floor." "*What*?!" The next thing I knew I read thirty-seven chapters. We tried to incorporate that feeling into the show as well, so that every episode ends with an "oh-my-God-what's-going-to-happen" moment so that you just keep watching. I've closed myself in a room and watched twelve hours of TV in one day. There is something kind of great about that. It's like spending a weekend with a really good book if it's something that you really like. I think that has changed a lot what television series are—especially the cable series that don't have commercial breaks. Regarding Michele Bachmann, that is some crazy business. That is some new crazy. There will be something in Season Five that is loosely influenced by Michele Bachmann. When you see some epic crazy like that, you have to use it.

Q: When you were directing and writing the finale of *Six Feet Under*, in what stage of the process did Sia's song ["Breath Me"] come into the mix. Was it written and directed with that in mind?
A: I knew that the final montage was going to be set to a song. The music supervisor that I work with—Gary Calamar who is really gifted—came in with a CD with ten different songs. That one seemed to make the most sense. When we filmed, we knew we would be using that, and we edited to that. It wasn't until after the episode was written until he brought that in. It was planned.

Q: *Six Feet Under* had all of these amazing death sequences. There was one in particular with a guy who walked into an office space and killed everyone. I remember it was quite controversial in Australia when it was on the air. I wonder how you deal with censorship and how often you get complaints because your work is so true and extremely violent, and it has a lot of sex in it. How do you get that on the air? How has that changed over the course of your career? Is it getting easier to get that on the air? Or is that something you worry about?
A: Again, it's HBO. You don't have the same issues you would have on another network. There were a rash of office shootings around that time in America. If I remember correctly, that's when the show had been on the air enough so that we were at the point where we were trying to find the ways to ramp up the expectation of the opening death moment where you think something was going to happen but then something else happened. That one was set up where the guy was on the phone and he had turned on the gas and he had lit a cigarette. So the impetus of that was to surprise the audience with an unexpected death.

But in terms of censorship, the biggest note I got on *Six Feet Under* was in the final season after Nate had died. It was the episode where it was his funeral. Brenda was getting Maya dressed, and she sort of lost her temper and yelled at her. Two of the executives at HBO had just become mothers. They were like, "I hate that. I hate her for that. She is a terrible mother." "Yeah, but her husband just died after having sex with some woman. So get over it." And the great thing about HBO is that they were like, "Okay. We trust you."

Q: I have one final question for you. What do you want your funeral to be like?
A: I want it to be a party. I want the people who cared about me—if they're still alive—to get together, to get drunk, and cry and laugh and go on living because I will be dead, and I won't care.

INDEX

Printed in the United States
by Baker & Taylor Publisher Services